Madrid had at least retained the Inf
leaving appeared like a promise to Spa
be abandoned. But just then Murat, t
of the kingdom, gave an order and berlines harnessed with seven mules, barouches, calashes, bore the young princes to the frontier. A roar went up from the mob: 'They are kidnapping them! To arms!' – like the roar of a man bound hand and foot who sees the surgeon carry away his amputated leg. It was May 1st. In the course of the day, Murat showed himself on the balcony and was received with a volley of curses.

The next day, May 2nd (the glorious *Dos de Mayo*), French officers were insulted by a mob of excited Madrilenos who had slept badly; they had to be extricated by patrols. The Plaza Mayor was thronged by armed civilians; Polish lancers charged in the Calle d'Alcala, Spanish citizens were mown down. On the Plaza de Oriente French rifles were fired, French guns roared and the cannon-balls ploughed avenues through the crowd of patriots.

Two hours later, Madrid was organized for the insurrection. Every house had become a fortress: furniture, sacks of pepper and boiling oil poured down from the balconies on to the pro-French.

The general of the Imperial Guard fell dead, struck by a flower-pot. At the Puerta del Sol, women threw themselves at the heads of the horses or hamstrung them. In the suburbs, Madrilenos from the back streets leapt from behind at the red-coated mamelukes, tore them from the saddle and drew their blood. The exasperated French army began to slaughter blindly. All the inhabitants of the houses from whose windows shots had been fired were massacred. After riflemen had broken down the doors of a monastery, the heads of the decapitated monks rained down into the street....

On May 3rd, the French were masters of Madrid. Their military tribunal sat at the postmaster-general's headquarters. From dawn to dusk silent patriots, their shirts open at the neck, their hands tied behind their backs, were taken through the streets in open carts to be shot in groups, in rows, in heaps at the Retiro, at Casa del Campo, at la Montana del Principe Pio, at the convent of Jesus and the church of Bon Suceso, at the Porta de Segovia and at la Moncloa.
At the end of the day the tribunal no longer passed judgment: Murat had ordered that every citizen of Madrid found carrying arms should be executed on the spot.

Dumb with horror, Don Luis listened to this recital, piecing together its bloody fragments, losing his foothold in this sea of blood. He was watching the death of his dream.

'On the morning of May 2nd,' the gunner said, 'France was still our ally. But since the evening of that very day every Spaniard looks on her as the enemy.'

Paul Morand
The Flagellant of Seville, 1953

CONTENTS

GOYA
PAINTER OF TERROR AND SPLENDOUR

Jeannine Baticle

THAMES AND HUDSON

Goya was born on 30 March 1746 at Fuendetodos, a small village lying some fifty kilometres south-west of Saragossa, the capital of Aragon. His father, José Goya, established himself in the town as a master gilder – a fairly profitable occupation in Spain, where altarpieces, decorated with wooden and metal sculptures, were gilded from top to bottom.

CHAPTER 1

FRANCISCO GOYA, MAN OF ARAGON

The little village of Fuendetodos (right) lay in arid country and numbered barely a hundred inhabitants. Goya's mother soon left it for Saragossa, a busy commercial and artistic centre. This 17th-century painting of the city (left) is by Martínez del Mazo.

Such was José Goya's expertise that the canons of the Basilica of Nuestra Señora del Pilar, the great shrine of Saragossa, appointed him to oversee the quality of the gilding of all the sculptures on which a wide range of Aragonese artists were working at that time.

It is easy to imagine Francisco Goya as a child following his father, gazing with wonder at the team of architects, painters and sculptors who, since 1750, had been remodelling, restoring and decorating the gigantic Basilica. He must have dreamed of one day mounting the vast scaffolding, like the famous Spanish fresco painter Antonio González Velázquez, who in 1753 decorated the dome, painting nearly forty metres above ground, all on his own, as inspiration took him... From early childhood Goya knew exactly what he wanted to do; and at the age of fourteen he became apprentice to José Luzán Martinéz, at one time painter to the Court. It was at Luzán's studio that Goya first met Francisco Bayeu (1734–95).

Early in 1763 Bayeu, considered one of Spain's best artists, was made assistant to the German Anton Raphael Mengs (1728–79), Court Painter. In July Bayeu was admitted to the Academy of San Fernando in Madrid.

Tradition has it that in the early days of Christianity the Virgin Mary appeared at Saragossa to Saint James and gave him a pillar (*pilar*), symbol of the first church to be constructed in honour of Mary. The miraculous Virgin of the Pilar was from henceforth an object of pilgrimage and the Basilica (left) was rebuilt several times around the pillar.

Goya sees a way to fame: following Bayeu's example he applies for a scholarship to the Academy

On 4 December 1763 he entered the competition, which required him to draw the cast of a statue of Silenus. Goya detested plaster casts, and when the results were announced on 15 January 1764 he had obtained not a single vote. In 1766 he failed again. This time the subjects were drawn from Spanish history: there was nothing contemporary, nothing set in Aragon. Goya was uninspired. Bayeu, one of the judges, favoured traditional figures and academic work and would hardly have appreciated the spirited daubs

of the young competitor. The first prize went to Bayeu's younger brother Ramón; Goya would not be formally admitted to the Academy until 5 July 1780.

While Goya and his fellows were busy with academic competitions, the famous *motin*, or uprising, of Esquilache took place in March 1766, part of a widespread rebellion in Spain provoked by the prohibition against wearing the traditional hat and cape. The following year a struggle for power ensued between the various religious orders, and the Jesuits were expelled from Spain. The antagonism between the traditional clergy and the Catholic intelligentsia in Spain featured prominently in Goya's satirical drawings.

The lost years: between the ages of twenty and twenty-five, Goya's life is a mystery

Did he live in Madrid, in the shadow of Francisco Bayeu, who was appointed Court Painter in 1767, aged only

Until the first half of the 18th century, apprentice artists learned to paint in a master's studio. In 1752, when the Academy of San Fernando was established in Madrid, formal teaching replaced the private classes. The change caused problems: the new Academy prescribed imitation of the antique and Italian art, imposing aesthetic values on Spanish painters who were by nature rebellious. This drawing is a contemporary study of a model in the Academy by Michel-Ange Houasse.

thirty-three? In the 19th century Goya's life was much romanticized and he was portrayed as a tempestuous youth living a bohemian existence.

Goya himself, in letters to his childhood friend Martín Zapater, suggests a somewhat wild adolescence when he harks back to their days as 'swaggerers' and remarks that in order to go to heaven: 'we must mend our ways in the time left to us'. He also tells his trusty friend the Spanish poet and dramatist Leandro Fernández de Moratín (1760–1828) that 'in my day I knew how to fight bulls and, sword in hand, feared no one'.

❛Four young men are amusing themselves, one letting the bull into the enclosure, another making a pass with a cape, the others looking on.❜

Goya

In *La Novillada* (a bullfight with young bulls) Goya actually portrayed himself as a bullfighter, tall, strong, muscular. His zest and vitality, which probably earned him his reputation as a 'swaggerer', make him stand out from the stiff, elegant, pious Bayeu, the fragile Mengs, and the slight figure of the Italian painter, Giambattista Tiepolo.

Whatever the misdemeanours of his youth, he was nonetheless passionately interested in contemporary art. Tiepolo's frescos, painted between 1762 and 1770 in the Royal Palace in Madrid, were a major influence, in particular his masterpiece on the ceiling of the throne room, *Allegory of the Grandeur of the Spanish Monarchy*. Goya was perhaps the only artist of the period able to exploit Tiepolo's mastery of light and use of space, and the way in which he disposed his strong, ample forms, perfectly visible at a distance, rendered in bright, luminous colours.

In a time when palace walls were hung with tapestries, great painters were busy drawing the cartoons on which the woven works were based. The cartoon *La Novillada* (right; detail above) was painted in 1780 for the ante-chamber of the Prince of Asturias at the Pardo Palace. Goya was now handling his subjects with greater freedom: note the lively composition and natural attitudes.

In spring 1771 Goya was in Rome, though we do not know exactly when he left Spain. He had entered a competition organized by the Academy of Parma (ruled by the Infante Philip, brother of Charles III of Spain),

describing himself as Roman and a pupil of Bayeu. This time the subject of the painting had to be taken from Antiquity. The results were published on 27 June 1771: the first and only prize was awarded to Paolo Borroni for the 'delicate harmony of the colouring'; Goya was criticized for the 'jarring tones' of his canvas, though the 'quality of grandeur' in the attitude of Hannibal was acknowledged. Goya's unorthodox work continued to shock advocates of orderly academic painting for some years. He won six votes, but no prize.

In October 1771 we again find mention of Goya's name in Saragossa. He receives his first commissions

Having acquired a certain reputation, probably because of his period in Rome, Goya came to the notice of the Chapter of the Pilar. They asked him to produce sketches for the ceiling of the small choir in the Chapel of the Virgin, opposite the miraculous chapel built by the architect Ventura Rodríguez. The subject was *The Adoration of the Name of God by Angels.* In early November Goya submitted a painting in fresco to show his grasp of the technique. The work was approved by the Chapter and on 11 November 1771 the canons confirmed the commission, the more readily because his fee was only 15,000 reals, whereas Antonio González Velázquez wanted 25,000 for the same task; 15,000 reals was a large sum for a beginner, equivalent to the annual salary of a Court Painter. On 27 January 1772 he submitted his sketches for the ceiling. They were greatly admired by the canons who asked him to start painting right away.

Tiepolo, born in Venice in 1696, died in Madrid in 1770, is regarded as the greatest European decorative artist of the 18th century. It was he who really brought the light of the sun into painting. His compositions have an amplitude and solidity of form and an understanding of perspective that strongly influenced Goya. Tiepolo had been commissioned to decorate the ceiling of the throne room in the Royal Palace in Madrid with an *Allegory of the Grandeur of the Spanish Monarchy* (signed and dated 1764); the astonishing use of perspective, the boldness of the attitudes and the three-dimensional power of the figures make this one of the artist's masterpieces. The frieze running round the ceiling features countrymen of the different regions of Spain and their produce, and the natives of Hispanic America (detail right). The mixture of allegory and realism must have impressed the young Goya.

The Statue of the Danube (left) is part of Giovanni Bernini's Fountain of the Four Rivers, in the Piazza Navona, Rome.

Goya was twenty-five; fortune was smiling on him at last. On 1 July 1772 the scaffolding was ready to come down. Goya's first fresco was complete. While influenced by Corrado Giaquinto (the Italian master of González Velázquez), the work clearly showed his own developing genius, attracting much attention from Aragonese high society.

Goya was next asked to decorate the oratory of the Palace of Sobradiel (some of the paintings there have since been destroyed); and he was taken under the wing of the canon Ramón Pignatelli, one of a distinguished Aragonese family, a kindly giant whose portrait he was to paint in 1791. Furthermore, Francisco Bayeu now held Goya in sufficiently high regard to give him his sister Josefa's hand in marriage. (Bayeu had himself brought up his orphaned brothers, Manuel and Ramón, who also became painters, and his two sisters.) In July 1773 Goya married Josefa Bayeu, known as 'Pepa', in Madrid. She was twenty-six, and he twenty-seven.

Through his brother-in-law Manuel, Goya was commissioned by the monks of the Carthusian Church of Aula Dei, some twelve kilometres north-west of Saragossa, to decorate it with paintings of the life of the Virgin. Between 1772 and 1774 Goya completed eleven great compositions. Only seven, heavily restored, survive today, but they nonetheless give a fair impression of the whole.

This bright, well composed fresco, *The Adoration of the Name of God by Angels*, clearly visible from the ground, already typifies Goya's work in its monumental forms, and the relatively few figures, which render the action more coherent. Another of Goya's best effects is seen in the strong, rounded faces with the lighting directly applied onto the red ochre preparation, without modelling, exactly re-creating the contours of forehead, nose, chin.

The 15th-century Church of Aula Dei was damaged in 1809, but Goya's paintings were restored. In some of the figures (left: detail of *The Visitation*), one already finds light laid over shadow like a mask, as in the later 'Black Paintings'.

Highly regarded in Saragossa, Goya now wants to conquer Madrid

He took advantage of the return of Mengs, who was responsible for overseeing the execution of the cartoons for the tapestries destined for the Royal Palace, to get himself known in the capital. He appears to have settled there definitively in 1775, the year in which his correspondence with Zapater began. The letters are intimate, and reveal a Goya who is impulsive, humorous, sometimes crude, always financially interested; money features large in his concerns and Zapater, a shrewd businessman, gives him good advice. Goya dislikes being in debt and is scrupulous about repaying what he owes. Zapater sends him chocolate, which the painter adores; Pepa chooses dresses and shawls for her Saragossa friends; not a week goes by without carriers taking or bringing cases of clothes, sweetmeats, wines, sometimes even a gundog – shooting was the favourite sport of Goya, Zapater and their mutual friend Juan Martín Goicoechea. A remarkable shot, Goya recounts his success with the gun: he kills partridges like flies and hares like tame rabbits. Numerous letters discuss the qualities of blunderbusses, and the gunsmith is often consulted. In the course of the correspondence a thoroughly endearing personality emerges, the portrait of a complete man, with passions and failings, generous, enthusiastic, full of insight and a tremendous love of life.

In Madrid painters frequent the Court and high society: for a long time Goya is ill at ease in these circles

The first royal commissions, in 1775, were cartoons for a series of tapestries for the dining room of the Prince of Asturias (the future Charles IV) in the Escorial. They represent hunting scenes and show a curious duality: a certain stiffness of execution – even at the peak of his maturity and success Goya painted official canvases more meticulously than private ones – is combined with remarkable precision of gesture, action and incidental detail. Bayeu, jealous of Goya, told the Royal Tapestry Factory that he was responsible for five of the cartoons; but Goya, in his bill, claimed to be solely responsible.

Paid 8000 reals for his work, Goya was for the moment content; however he soon grew frustrated at having to express his talent in the form of textiles. At the end of the year he put in a bill for *The Picnic*, noting 'the composition is of my design'. The cartoon was for a series of tapestries to hang in the dining room of the Prince of Asturias in the Pardo. In 1776–8 nine other paintings followed, among them Goya's first masterpieces, *The Dance on the Banks of the Manzanares*, *The Brawl at the New Tavern*, *The Maja and the Masked Men*, *The Kite*, and *The Parasol* (directly influenced by Tiepolo), to cite the most important. Each embodied qualities that were essentially painterly: a sense of space, of light, the realism of social types, attitudes and costumes, skilful composition, plasticity of form, warmth and colour, in the distinctive style of the artist. No other painter in Europe has to such an extent raised the events of everyday life to the level of historical composition without losing any of its naturalness and gaiety.

❛ Friend, your last letter was a knife in my heart: you can't imagine how I envy you the moment you mention shooting.... For me there is no greater pleasure in the world. I have only managed to get away once and yet no one has done better: 19 shots, 18 hits: to be precise 2 hares, 1 rabbit, 4 young partridges, 1 old partridge and 10 quails. The shot I missed was a partridge. I particularly enjoyed my good luck, having set out with two of the best guns in the place. I won a certain reputation with them.❜

Letter to Zapater

The Escorial (above), a granite monastery and palace, is also a museum housing the royal collections.

Productive years: two events, one private, one public, in Goya's life

On 21 January 1777 his son Vicente Anastasio was born in Madrid. The proud and delighted father informed Zapater 'Pepa has given birth to a fine boy'; alas, like most of his siblings, he died young.

That year marked a change in the political landscape: the new head of government brought a return to nationalism. Charles III, who had ascended the Spanish throne in 1759, favoured foreign politicians, particularly Italians. But at the end of 1776 he agreed to get rid of the Genoese minister Grimaldi, and replace him, to the fury of the aristocracy, with José Moniño, Count of Floridablanca – an ex-magistrate. The Spanish nobility considered a minister chosen from the ranks of the lawyers to be barely preferable to a foreigner.

It was, however, from the lawyers, highly regarded in Spain, that the *ilustrados* were predominantly recruited. These were 'enlightened' intellectuals who wanted to take their country out of the Middle Ages, in which it was in many respects still rooted, and into the modern world. Their leader, Pedro de Campomanes, was a remarkable economist and lawyer, and a friend of the Count of Floridablanca. Campomanes was closely associated with a young magistrate then posted in Seville, Gaspar Melchor de Jovellanos, one of the figureheads of liberal thought at the time. A great influence on the artist, he reappears throughout Goya's life.

King Charles III (1716–88), fourth son of Philip V of Bourbon, ascended the throne in 1759. He enjoyed great moral status and was regarded as the king of 'enlightened Spain'. This portrait of him in hunting attire dates from 1786 to 1788.

Floridablanca, now Secretary of State, assembled a group of technocrats (as we would say today), aiming to recruit the best available minds. Elegant, distinguished, descended from a noble Asturian family, Jovellanos was appointed chief justice in Madrid in October 1778. Lover of the fine arts, poet and dramatist, he became a member of the Academy of History and the Academy of San Fernando (1780) and was one of the most brilliant figures in Campomanes' Madrid *soirées*, at which the cultural elite used to gather. There Jovellanos met Goya, the engraver Pedro González Sepulveda, and Francisco de Cabarrús, the evil genius of his career. The latter was then but a young Basque trader, based in Madrid, father of the six-year-old Teresa who became famous under the name Mme Tallien during the French Revolution.

In *The Brawl at the New Tavern* or *La Venta Nueva* (above), Goya pictures an inn 'where postilions and muleteers arrive from several Spanish provinces, and settle to play cards: a man from Murcia is assailed by two companions and a fight ensues.' Spanish inns had indeed a generally bad reputation. Many travellers complained of them in their writings.

Goya was now in his thirties. The talented son of a craftsman and an illiterate countrywoman was entering a remarkable social circle, very different from that of the court. This was the world of the *ilustrados*, 'enlightened' historians, thinkers, economists, writers, who discussed problems of great interest and moment, and sought to combat the traditional ills of Spain.

CHAPTER 2

SPAIN IN THE TIME OF THE *ILUSTRADOS*

Influenced by the *ilustrados*, Goya handled subjects of topical concern: the power of Church versus State, the backwardness of culture and industry, beggars, delinquency, madness. Left: a self-portrait (1783). Right: an engraving from *The Caprices* (1799).

These men taught him to think and give form to his ideas, to see the complexity of human life. They sowed the seeds of his later work, *The Caprices.* Goya was already interested in engraving – he was one of the few painters of his time to excel in both media – and got permission to make etchings of the works of the greatest painter of the Spanish school, Diego Velázquez (1599–1660), whose works had recently been moved to the Palacio Nuevo, the present Royal Palace in Madrid, completed in 1765.

While the works of many artists were engraved in their lifetime, Velázquez had to wait for Goya. The publication of plates after the paintings of Velázquez was announced in the *Gaceta de Madrid* in July and December 1778. Goya sent a set to Zapater, adding that they 'have caused me a thousand problems', but they were now in the hands of the King. One has to imagine the young painter, Goya, discovering in the work of the older master his characteristic 'magic of atmosphere'; his way of using a blob of paint, impasto, to create the illusion of a face, of an iridescent material, or a jewel; his transparency of tone; and his restrained palette – ochres, white, black, very little red and blue – that yet conveys, through a skilful use of glaze, the impression of an infinite variety of colour, and the sense that the figure represented was living and breathing. Goya achieved the impossible by re-creating in black and white, solely by his etcher's burin, the supreme economy of Velázquez's pictorial techniques; he later said: 'I had three masters: Rembrandt, Velázquez and nature.'

In the 1780s Goya's blossoming career took him into the drawing rooms of the Royal Palace, where Velázquez reigned supreme, and those of Campomanes, where Jovellanos and Cabarrús were already beginning to shine.

Velázquez painted *Las Meninas* (right), formerly entitled *The Family of Philip IV*, in 1656. In the centre is the little Infanta Margarita, aged five, with her ladies-in-waiting (the *meninas*). The artist included himself in the painting, on the left in front of a huge canvas. It is a major masterpiece, combining realism and a sense of poetry, a brilliant illusion that draws the viewer into a living present. Goya's etching (detail below) captures the atmosphere.

The heir to the throne Charles and his wife the Infanta María Luisa are delighted with their apartments in the Pardo Palace, redecorated by Goya

The superb, youthful figures of the *majos* and buxom *majas*, the fine gentlemen, the charming children, were depicted delightfully by Goya, who between 1778 and 1780 executed seven cartoons of tapestries for the bedroom and thirteen for the antechamber. The daily life of the Spanish people was enacted before their eyes: *The Washerwomen*, *The Crockery Seller*, *The Doctor*, *The Game of Pelota* – far more arresting than the banal, outdated tapestries made after paintings by the Flemish painter David Teniers. The Prince and Princess preferred contemporary art to any other and, had they lived in the 20th century, would probably have appointed Pablo Picasso as Court Painter.

Their taste accorded well with Goya's developing talent. On 9 January 1779 he joyfully announced that he had presented four paintings to the King, the Prince of Asturias and his wife: '[He] kissed their hand and had never known such great happiness.' They, in turn, expressed their appreciation.

After some while, he thought that the time had come to ask for the position of Court Painter, which was refused him. One suspects that Bayeu was reluctant to see his young brother-in-law hold the same post as himself; after Mengs had departed for Italy, Bayeu became regarded as First Court Painter and enjoyed the protection of the King's confessor, the Franciscan Father Eleta. Bayeu's graceful work, impeccable presentation and light colours were in sharp contrast to Goya's vivacity and grandiose style, which largely explained their differences and aesthetic incompatibility.

According to Goya, the *Crockery Seller*, or *El Cacharrero* (opposite) came from Valencia. The artist was in no way attempting a realistic portrayal of the *rastro* – the popular open air market: the carriage passing behind is distinctly theatrical, while the footman at the rear might have come straight out of a comedy. The coach-driver, portrayed from behind, and the poetic figure of the lady show an artistry that is all his own.

The Pardo Palace, shown in this 19th-century engraving, had been a royal residence from the Middle Ages. Fourteen kilometres from Madrid on the road to La Corunna, it was built under the Emperor Charles V (Charles I of Spain) and substantially enlarged under Charles III, which explains the numerous commissions Goya received for tapestry cartoons for its rooms.

MADRID

Goya possessed a fascinating blend of genius and practicality; he had already built up a capital of 100,000 reals (a gardener earned at the most 350 reals per year) and asked Zapater for advice on how best to invest his money.

Materially secure, professionally acclaimed, Goya anticipates a promising future. But in 1781 he is to suffer the greatest humiliation of his career – in Saragossa

The Chapter of the Pilar had for some time been asking to see Goya. In May 1780, when financial problems put a stop to the work of the Royal Tapestry Factory, he offered them his services. Through the agency of Bayeu, a contract in the sum of 60,000 reals was agreed for the painting of a single dome.

Madrid changed greatly in appearance in the 18th century, thanks to the works undertaken by the Spanish Bourbons. Streets were opened up and civil and religious buildings erected, as well as customs houses, hospitals, academies, the Basilica of San Francisco el Grande and the Church of the Salesians. The charm of the city, with its population of 150,000 inhabitants, lay in its squares and its majestic bridges. This watercolour of the Toledo Bridge is by the Scottish artist David Roberts (1796–1864).

On 5 October 1780 Goya, now back in Saragossa, presented two sketches to the works committee of the Pilar; they were accepted and he was free to begin. He must indeed have been pleased that the dreams of his youth were being realized. The base of the dome was twenty-eight metres from the ground, opposite the Chapel of Saint Joachim; it had a diameter of twelve metres and the surface to be painted covered 212 square metres. Like all good fresco artists, Goya worked at extraordinary speed; he completed the whole fresco in forty-one sessions, which took him four months, including the time taken for preparation. On 14 December 1780, however, two months into the project, trouble began. Bayeu, who was painting another dome while at the same time overseeing the whole project, informed Canon Allué, administrator of works at Pilar, that Goya had refused to make the corrections he wanted. The Canon, in his turn, then identified 'defective areas' in Goya's fresco himself, and decided that Goya had not been sufficiently appreciative of his brother-in-law. On 11 February 1781 the culprit was summoned and told to finish the decoration of the dome by presenting sketches for the pendentives. In March the canons rejected these sketches as 'unfinished' and 'showing the same faults' as the fresco in their 'colours, attitudes and the arrangement of the drapery'; '*Charity* is not as decent as she should be'; 'the background of the other sketches is too dark and lacking in detail'. Allué advised that Goya be made to correct the mistakes in the fresco 'which have aroused the censure of the public' – a poor excuse, since only Bayeu and his assistants were authorized to climb the dizzying heights of the scaffolding, and from below no one could judge the quality of the drapery and brushstrokes. Clearly Bayeu was pouring oil on the fire – although he himself would paint a dome as if it were an easel picture, so that from the ground it is impossible to make out the shapes in his frescos at the Pilar. Goya was furious and protested strongly to the Pilar administration, pleading the creative freedom of the artist. He arrogantly refused to comply with the wishes of Bayeu, whose role in this whole affair is indeed extremely discreditable.

A fresco must be painted on wet plaster and each section finished before the plaster dries. This means the work has to be carefully planned in advance. At each session the artist can cover three or four square metres but has to take care that the separate sections meet neatly. The number of sections demarcated is often an indication of the number of days it took the artist to paint the fresco.

It grew so heated that the Carthusian Felix Salcedo, a friend of Goya, intervened to restore calm and bring him to reason: the artist made the corrections required by his exigent brother-in-law and finished the dome. On 29 May 1781 Canon Allué authorized the payment of the remaining 45,000 reals owing to Goya and was incensed by his lack of courtesy when they met. On 30 May, the instant he was paid, Goya went back to Madrid with his family. So angry was he with Bayeu and the Aragonese clergy that he kept away from his native province for a long time. 'The memory of Saragossa and the painting burns me alive', he later told Zapater.

Goya's fresco paved the way for the audacities of the dome of San Antonio de la Florida painted nearly twenty years later. Its bold composition and its command of perspective and technique made it a masterpiece. He had learned the lesson of his great predecessors in Rome, particularly Michelangelo (1475–1564), realizing that figures thirty metres above ground should not be presented in the same way as those to be seen at eye-level. The celestial world created by Goya, at once 'courtly and popular', circulates with natural ease round the *Virgin in Glory*, whose superb countenance radiates majesty, and testifies to the artist's deep faith.

Goya was perhaps the only artist in his time to rival Tiepolo; but the Aragonese clergy, more patrons of religion than lovers of art, failed to appreciate the fact.

As soon as he is back in Madrid Goya takes dazzling revenge

Fortunately he had had supporters in the capital for some years, among them his friend Juan Martín Goicoechea, a close associate of the all-powerful Canon Pignatelli, who was most influential at Court. On 25 July 1781 he informed Zapater in triumph: 'His Majesty has decided that paintings should be executed' to decorate the chapels of the Church of San Francisco el Grande in Madrid, and that he had been chosen for the purpose with 'the great Bayeu' and Mariano de Maëlla. The church had been under reconstruction since 1760, the architect in charge being Francisco Sabatini, from whom Goya took his orders on Court commissions. The subject of the painting was a scene from the life of Saint Bernardino of Siena. At the end of August 1781 Goya began his sketch: *Saint Bernardino of Siena Preaching to Alfonso V of Aragon.* Shortly after, he showed it to Floridablanca who seems to have been supervising the project. Goya wrote to him explaining his work, whose narrow format (roughly five by three metres) made the composition difficult. As usual he was concerned with use of space. On 11 January 1783 the paintings were installed in San Francisco el

Recent discoveries of archive material, radiographic studies and the publication of little-known works have radically transformed our understanding of Goya's art. Colour photographs of details of the fresco in the Pilar (left; detail below), published only in 1983, have at last made it possible for their remarkable quality to be appreciated. Had the dome of the Pilar been as easily visible as that of San Antonio de la Florida, which is only ten metres above the ground, art historians would doubtless long ago have recognized that Goya's genius was manifest from his youth.

Grande, but only on 8 December 1784 did the King at last visit the new church. Three days later Goya was inundated with congratulations; the work is, however, a little disappointing, if excellent in parts. (Goya portrayed himself, with radiant face, on the left of the fresco and the image so pleased him that he based a self-portrait on it.)

The patronage of Jovellanos played an important part in Goya's life in the 1780s. In the same period Cabarrús became more powerful. In 1782 he was authorized to create the first national bank of Spain, the Bank of San Carlos. Jovellanos was brought in to audit the Central American accounts; and Goya placed money in the new bank, as he 'had a few friends there'.

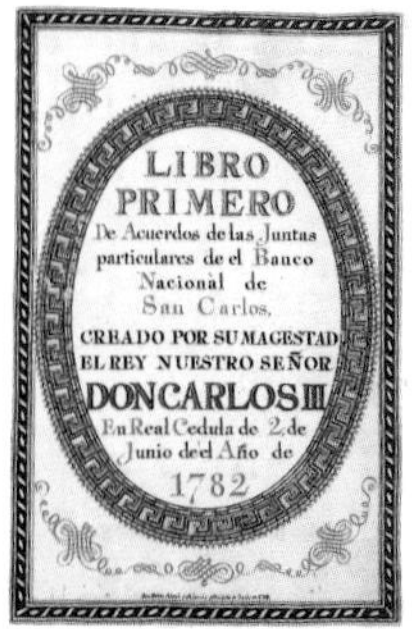

LIBRO
PRIMERO
De Acuerdos de las Juntas
particulares de el Banco
Nacionàl de
San Carlos,
CREADO POR SU MAGESTAD
EL REY NUESTRO SEÑOR
DON CARLOS III
En Real Cedula de 2 de
Junio de el Año de
1782

The National Bank of San Carlos was established in 1782 by Cabarrús, whose patrons were Muzquiz, the Count of Gausa, Finance Minister, and the Count of Floridablanca. Distinguished figures such as the Count of Altamira, the Duke of Alba's brother-in-law, were part of the management. The Bank was highly successful in Europe in its first years. Above is the cover of its first report.

In late January 1783 he was commissioned to paint the portrait of the Count of Floridablanca. Portraiture played an important role in Goya's work, enabling him to study the character and temperament of each of his models with minute scrutiny. He has left us an astonishing collection which, in its systematic observation, has the psychological range and insight found in the novels of Balzac or Dickens.

The progress of Floridablanca's portrait can be followed in Goya's letters; on 26 April he painted the head from life: 'it is very like'. It was essential to make it a true likeness; there was to be no question of beautifying or modifying his unattractive features. A certain stiffness of attitude, a chiaroscuro unsuited to the composition and the ill-assorted colours show the awkwardness Goya felt tackling an official portrait; his taste for realism conflicted with the need for decorum, though soon he would learn to reconcile the two requirements.

The rise of a portrait painter

Early the following year he was suffering some disappointment at finding that Floridablanca had forgotten him. 'Goya, we shall see each other later', the Count had said, perhaps less satisfied with his portrait than the artist supposed.

But Goya was infinitely resilient; instead of brooding on his disappointments he found other patrons no less

Don José Moñino, Count of Floridablanca (1728–1808), a lawyer who rose to ministerial rank, attracted early notice through his qualities as a jurist. In 1772 he was Spanish ambassador in Rome. In 1777 he was appointed Secretary of State, the equivalent of Prime Minister. He had to overcome the opposition of the Spanish aristocracy in order to bring in reforms that placed him in the front rank of the *ilustrados* in Spain. The repercussions of the French Revolution on Spanish politics brought about his fall in 1792. Goya painted this portrait of him in 1783, when a commission from a man of his rank was an important achievement. He reported it to his friend Zapater under oath of secrecy: only his wife Josefa had been informed. He said that he had spent two hours after dinner with the statesman, adding that he had not solicited the commission of which he was so proud. In the long periods they spent painting the portraits of public figures, artists such as Goya gained access to a fascinating world, and were on occasion privy to political secrets.

distinguished. These included the Infante Don Luis, younger brother of Charles III, who in 1776, aged forty-nine, had morganatically married a ravishing seventeen-year-old girl from Aragon, María Teresa Vallabriga. Forced by this misalliance to remove himself from the Court, he maintained several residences. One, at Arenas de San Pedro, on the southern slope of the Gredos mountains, some eighty kilometres west of Madrid, was a paradise; the architect Domingo Tomás began to build a great palace there, never finished. On 20 September 1783 Goya wrote telling Zapater that he was coming back from Arenas de San Pedro exhausted: 'His Highness behaved very graciously, I painted his portrait, his wife's, the little boy's and the little girl's with unexpected success, four other painters did not succeed.' He spent a month at Arenas de San Pedro, and twice went hunting with Don Luis. His host gave him 1000 douros (20,000 reals) and a dressing gown for his wife, covered in silver and gold, that was said to be worth 30,000 reals.

The architect Ventura Rodríguez (above) was painted by Goya in 1784 standing in front of a symbolic pillar. He is holding his plan of the miraculous chapel of the Pilar, which has just been built.

Goya's letter enables the portraits of Don Luis and his family to be precisely dated. Two studies in profile of Don Luis and his wife bear the date and duration of the work on the back: three hours on each occasion. It is hard to judge the quality of the portraits of Don Luis and María Teresa Vallabriga as they have not survived in their original state. Those of the children, however, are very appealing – the girl set against a magnificent mountain background, the boy dressed very prettily in blue.

In October 1784 Goya returned to Arenas and the Infante paid him 30,000 reals for two paintings: very probably the *Portrait of María Teresa Vallabriga on Horseback* and the exceptional *Family of the Infante Don Luis*, one of Goya's first masterpieces. It was probably at this time too that Don Luis asked Goya to paint Ventura Rodríguez, his favourite architect. The portrait is a fine and important work, in harmonious shades of grey; Goya seems for the first time to forget the social rank of his model and conveys not only the physical appearance of the architect but also his psychological qualities.

The year 1784 was a very full one for Goya. In the first six months he did four paintings (later destroyed in the Napoleonic Wars), commissioned at the instigation of Jovellanos for the college of Calatrava at Salamanca.

Doña María Teresa Vallabriga y Rozas married the King's brother Don Luis of Bourbon in 1776. Having a deep devotion to the Virgin of the Pilar she gave the treasury of the Church a diamond ornament that had been a wedding present from her husband. Goya painted this equestrian portrait of her (right) in 1784.

In *The Family of the Infante Don Luis* Goya takes us into the intimate world of the Prince and his immediate circle. He is playing cards, his two eldest sons gathered round him, while his wife has her hair done by candlelight and the youngest child is in the arms of her nurse. The composition is handled like a Rembrandt night scene: Goya had perfectly absorbed the master's way of realizing half-light, warm and coloured, but brushed, in generous applications with little impasto, in the romantic manner.

Don Luis (in profile in the centre of the painting) had been made a cardinal at the age of eight. In 1746 he abandoned his clerical habit and embarked on a somewhat debauched existence. His marriage to María Teresa Vallabriga made him settle down and introduced him to the joys of family life. The little girl on the left, near the painter, is the Countess Chinchón, later married off to Godoy. In 1800 she was the subject of one of Goya's most beautiful portraits.

His private life also flourishes during the decade

From 1779 Goya lived with his family at 1 Calle del Desengaño, in a steep quarter of north-east Madrid, one of the oldest and most charming parts of the city, alas now partly destroyed. He lived there until he left for France in 1824, a period of some forty-five years, moving only once, in 1800, to the second floor of the house opposite, on the corner of the Calle del Desengaño and the pretty Calle Valverde. In 1795 the Duchess of Alba was to visit the studio of the painter's first house, to have her face made-up to look healthier, while the Duke of Wellington was to sit for his portrait in the second house, in 1812; the district is haunted by distinguished ghosts.

The legend of the Calle del Desengaño, where Goya lived, is very poetic. In the 16th century a young gentleman was courting a lady who lived in this deserted district. One night he saw four men pursuing a shadow veiled in white and followed on their heels. When they caught up with the shadow and tore off its veil they found a corpse and cried out: '*Quel desengaño!*' ('What a disillusion!')

It was at l Calle del Desengaño that a son, Francisco Javier, was born to Goya and his wife on 2 December 1784, their only child to survive. 'Let us hope this one will get a chance to grow', sighed Goya, with Josefa very ill after the birth.

Goya's correspondence with Zapater rarely mentions political events (his letters were later censored by Zapater's nephew), but in January 1785 he reported the death of the finance minister Muzquiz, Cabarrús' protector. The latter was now at the mercy of the new minister, his worst enemy, Pedro de Lerena – a hard, industrious man who supervised the works of the Court and adversely affected Goya's career.

Goya's engraving *The Blind Man with a Guitar* (1778) portrays the Plaza de la Cebada where the famous Madrid fairs were held (not far from San Francisco el Grande); the figure of the blind man foreshadows the later 'Black Paintings'. This is the only tapestry cartoon that Goya engraved himself – probably one of his first engravings and in any case the largest. Fewer than a dozen copies are known. In his engravings after Velázquez the same year, Goya first explored the possibilities of aquatint, a recently invented engraving technique imitating wash drawing.

In 1785 Goya meets the Marquis and Marquise of Peñafiel, future Duke and Duchess of Osuna, his most faithful patrons for thirty years

The Marquise of Peñafiel, Countess of Benavente, was one of the most remarkable

women in Spanish high society. Exquisitely elegant, cultivated, a good mother, she befriended musicians, poets, artists and actors. Goya quickly became her favourite painter and she commissioned him to paint her and her husband in 1785. The *Portrait of the Countess of Benavente* imitates, down to the dress itself, that of Queen Marie-Antoinette by the French painter Elisabeth Vigée-Lebrun (1755–1842). Goya avoided the pitfalls of painting subjects within the context of courtly artificiality: the work is a dazzling exercise by a colourist, a harmony of blue, green, grey and pink. It established Goya as the best portraitist of his age. From now on, he could paint kings and bullfighters with equal realism. Of

Bullfighting greatly interested Goya and was the subject of a number of his works, including this *Bullfight in a Village* (1793–4) and a series of etchings published in 1816. He portrayed the two most famous bullfighters of his time, Costillares and Pedro Romero (far right). The latter was a popular idol and a protégé of the Duke and Duchess of Osuna.

course he also went shooting with the Marquis of Peñafiel, telling Zapater that he was 'remarkable and remarked upon' for the size of his bag.

The moment had come to seek official favours. On 2 February 1785 he applied for the post of deputy director of painting at the Academy of San Fernando, which he obtained on 4 May. He promised to visit Zapater in August, after finishing a portrait for Lerena, then changed his mind and went for a fortnight's shooting at Chinchón, a pretty village outside Madrid where his brother Camilo was chaplain; their mother Gracia Lucientes, who had been very close to Goya, died in 1785 – their father had died in 1781.

❛It has been said and repeated on all sides that the taste for bullfights was dying out in Spain, and that civilization would soon cause them to disappear; if it does, so much the worse for civilization, for a bullfight is one of the finest spectacles that the imagination of man could devise; but this day is still far off, and the tender-hearted writers who assert the contrary have only to be transported one Monday, between four and five o'clock, to the Puerta de Alcal, in order to convince themselves that the taste for this "cruel" amusement is still far from extinct.❜

Théophile Gautier
Wanderings in Spain
1845

In his forties Goya achieves total freedom of expression

This was the fruit of relentless effort, the will to conquer his weak points. Another shadow over this idyllic period was the death in 1785 of the Infante Don Luis. From him Goya had learned that tolerance and generosity are prerogatives of the great also.

Notwithstanding the loss of his great patron, the artist's career was launched, and the year 1786 proved equally productive. Goya's talent was now fully developed; his subsequent work was not better, but different. Indeed the quality that most makes him unique was the remarkable ability to adapt his style to changing circumstances, people, things, each time seeming to add something new. Now his art conveyed the charm of the last years of 'the sweetness of life'; later it would unflinchingly catalogue the horrors of war.

Success brings money, but never enough to satisfy Goya

He claimed that his income from the bank and the Academy amounted to only 12,000 or 13,000 reals a year. Fortunately, on 25 June 1786, he was appointed Court Painter at a fixed annual salary of 15,000 reals. He soon bought, for 7000 reals, a *birlocho*, a little English two-wheeled carriage 'all gilded and varnished, which people stopped to look at'. Both horse and carriage overturned in the ditch on the first outing. By some miracle Goya escaped with only a minor injury to his ankle.

His appointment as Court Painter may have helped to reconcile Goya and Bayeu (who boasted it was got through his agency). In 1786 Goya painted a magnificent portrait of Bayeu in subdued,

Charles III introduced legislation to protect the Spanish workers. He commissioned Goya to paint *The Wounded Mason* as a visual record of his resolve to better their economic situation. Sensitive to the ills and sufferings of his fellow man, Goya injected a striking note of drama into the scene.

sumptuous red-brown tones, which was executed with astonishing freedom.

His main task at Court was to paint more tapestry cartoons, and in the summer of 1786 he was commissioned to design a new series for the dining room at the Pardo Palace. On 12 September he told Zapater he was working on sketches. The following autumn he presented them at the Escorial to the King and Infantes, who expressed their satisfaction. The sketches were a marvel: *Spring*, *Summer*, *Winter*, followed by *The Wounded Mason* and *The Poor at the Fountain* – conventional subjects given new life by Goya's fresh, spontaneous vision. The cartoons painted from these sketches now number among Goya's most famous works: the realism of *Autumn*, of the harvest in the golden light of *Summer*, of *Winter* iciness, perfectly balances the stylization of decorative art. He employs a wider colour range than usual, light, transparent, perfectly conveying a sense of volume. Goya had learnt from Velázquez how to vary the colouring in light to obtain maximum relief without violently contrasting light and shade.

One gets the impression that painting was always in his thoughts: even out shooting he must automatically have registered the play of form and colour in a country scene, which he then re-created on canvas.

Intense activity: winter 1786–7

He painted portraits for the Bank of San Carlos: the *Count of Altamira*, an extraordinary ill-made puppet, and *King Charles III*, a man of legendary ugliness, stiffly portrayed, perhaps because Goya felt constrained in his presence. Working on the series throughout the year, he finished with a portrait of *Cabarrús* (see p. 57).

In *The Poor at the Fountain* (1786–7) Goya again portrays the wretchedness of the people. Their King, like his 17th-century predecessors, wanted a constant reminder of their plight on his drawing-room walls. Goya conveys an intense feeling of cold, making more cruel the plight of its destitute victims.

The tapestry cartoons: a touch of the everyday

The Bourbon princes were reformers who believed that by presenting an optimistic view of ordinary people's lives, picturing their happiest moments, one could encourage the raising of living standards. For this reason Goya's tapestry cartoons should not be seen as realistic social portrayals of his age; on the contrary, one needs to recognize in them an element of propaganda, which Goya has invested with an astonishing vitality. Despite the artificial nature of the commission, he managed to avoid conventional representation, painting creatures of flesh and blood.

The most famous work in the series of cartoons entitled *The Four Seasons* (1786–7) is *Autumn* or *The Vintage* (left). Goya skilfully associates the elegant group in the foreground with the realism of the grape-harvest taking place behind, against the mountain background. In *Spring* or *The Flower Sellers* (far left) the young women in graceful attitudes are accompanied by a humorous figure who is going to surprise the girl with a rabbit.

The tapestry cartoons: the realities of working the land

In *Summer* or *The Harvest*, a vast composition three metres high by 3.6 metres wide, naturalism prevails. Goya represents a group of harvesters having a siesta, with an authentic flavour of country life that brings to mind the work, some sixty years later in date, of the 19th-century French artist Gustave Courbet. Here again it is the everyday realism of the natural world, not a theatrical version, that Goya portrays. Highly poetic, strikingly realistic, the cartoon is masterly in its execution and free rendering.

The tapestry cartoons: another image of nature

When he painted *Winter* or *The Snowstorm*, Goya must have remembered his native region and the rigours of the Aragonese winters. He conveys the impression that the cold is more intense, more piercing than elsewhere. His figures appear to be moving in a glaucous, grey-green universe. He seems to encompass everything in one comprehensive gaze.

Modern in its composition, the picture had no background scene. The financier, with his proverbial relaxed manner, dressed in yellow silk, probably disconcerted Goya, who preferred more tense and static sitters.

On 22 April 1787 Goya went to the Osunas' country house, the Alameda, to deliver seven canvases for the drawing room. His subjects were half rococo, half modern in inspiration: *The Fall from the Donkey* and *The Swing* appeared in all the boudoirs of Europe, while the game of *The Greased Pole*, the brutal *Attack on a Coach*, *Village Procession* and *Choosing the Bulls* (a lost work) were still more popular. All the colours were taken from the land of fairy tale and applied with the quickness of stroke and the feeling for light and space that became characteristic of Goya's art, and as effortless and natural to him as breathing.

Cabarrús was summoned to France to take up, so it was reported, an important financial position. He stayed in Paris from the end of April to August, accompanied by a young poet, Leandro de Moratín, who had been recommended to him as a secretary by Jovellanos and who was to become a close friend of Goya.

Did the painter intend to join them? In any case, he tried to learn French, and wrote to Zapater on 14 November. 'I am venturing, my dear friend, to write to you in French as I know that you love the language. I have taken it into my head to learn it.' Goya freely admits that he is sending his first efforts and also suggests that he forward his dictionary to him.

Earlier on, at the beginning of June 1787, he had advised his friend that for the feast of Saint Anne (26 July) three of his paintings of life-size figures, commissioned by order of the King, were to be installed in the Convent of Santa Ana in Valladolid, adorning the altarpieces.

These works represented *The Death of Saint Joseph*, *Saint Bernard* and *Saint Lutgardis*. 'At the moment, nothing has begun!' (he had five weeks left). Otherwise 'the mules are well, and so is the berlin which I've just tried'. He must have done the paintings very quickly, perhaps taking an assistant, not daring on a royal commission to work in the sketchy style that came most naturally to him. Interestingly the compositions have a neo-classical aspect unusual in his work.

He had much more success the following year in the two remarkable paintings ordered by the Duke and Duchess of Osuna in honour of their forebear Saint Francis of Borgia, to decorate the latter's votive chapel in Valencia Cathedral. He was paid 30,000 reals for them in instalments over two years. After the somewhat academic manner of his work for Santa Ana, he adopted a sort of 'troubadour' style for *Saint Francis of Borgia and his Family* – almost Venetian in touch and colouring – and a futuristic genre in *Saint Francis of Borgia and the Impenitent Dying Man* (the first appearance of the devil in his work, a look ahead to *The Caprices* and the 'Black Paintings'). The superb chiaroscuro recalls the works of Rembrandt, a frequent reference point of Goya's.

Goya developed towards greater gravity. Without taking too seriously his confidence to Zapater that he 'had grown old with lots of wrinkles' and that his friend 'would recognize him only by his snub nose and deep-set eyes', there is undoubtedly a core of truth in his confession.

Francisco Cabarrús (1752–1810), a brilliant financier and economist, played a very important role in Spain between 1780 and 1800. Goya painted the above portrait of him in 1787.

In 1788 Goya declares himself overloaded with work

On 31 May 1788 he wrote about a commission for the bedroom of the Infantes in the Pardo Palace, over which he was taking great care, as 'the King is to see it'. 'The subjects are very difficult and give great trouble, above all the Pradera de San Isidro on the saint's feast day, with all the habitual commotion of the place'. This view of Madrid, *The Meadow of Saint Isidro* was painted in 1788, ten years earlier than has been supposed (proof of the danger of dating Goya by his style). The superb panorama, in many ways heralding Corot a hundred years

According to Goya *The Greased Pole* (left) showed 'a maypole on the village green, with boys climbing up it to win the prize, consisting of chickens and cakes in the form of crowns hung from the top of the pole. People are watching them.'

later, brilliantly evokes the colours of the May sunset over Madrid, the same shimmering light over the landscape that is to be seen today.

Other prestigious commissions included the portrait of the *Countess of Altamira* (sister-in-law of the Duchess of Alba) and her daughter – a jewel, in arresting shades of blue and pink, which makes one think of Renoir – and also portraits of her sons the *Count of Trastamare* and the famous little boy in red, *Manuel Osorio*, at the age of three or four. Here Goya shows his total mastery of child portraiture, its charm, grace, candour. One senses his appreciation of the natural attitudes of children, their droll and tender qualities, no doubt observed in his own beloved son. Like Velázquez, he omits a background setting in his intimate portraits. The daringly composed *Portrait of the Duke and Duchess of Osuna with their Children* strikes a true note, avoiding any hint of affectation.

Charles III died in December 1788; the Prince of Asturias ascended the throne. The new king and queen were hardly grief-stricken, having ceaselessly plotted against the old monarch, who had kept them on a tight rein. Despite strict Court mourning – 'not so much black crêpe', Goya ironically pleaded – María Luisa was full of life. She began to introduce her favourites, starting with her lover, the young bodyguard Manuel Godoy, quickly promoted. Goya was appointed Court Painter on 30 April 1789, thanks to the patronage of Charles IV and Jovellanos, whose cousin, the Marquis of Valdecarzana, signed the nomination. Goya reported that he took his oath before Valdecarzana and the clerk with 'a great deal of authority'.

The feast of Saint Isidro was celebrated on 15 May. Goya's painting *The Meadow of Saint Isidro* portrayed the popular gathering on the right bank of the Manzanares opposite the Royal Palace and San Francisco el Grande, in front of the hermitage dedicated to the saint. It was in this district that Goya thirty years later bought the 'House of the Deaf Man'.

Goya painted the portrait of the Duke and Duchess of Osuna with their children (right) in 1788. The Duchess' first children had died, which is why the four shown are so young although she is thirty-six. The oldest child, Manuela, is five, the second, Joaquina, three (Goya later painted her portrait as the Marquise of Santa Cruz); Francisco Borgia is two, and Pedro de Alcántara one. It is a marvellous portrait in harmonious shades of grey, executed with particular care.

1

3

Goya, seen at work in this self-portrait of 1793–5 (1), differed from the traditional Court Painters in the relaxed manner with which he painted children. He saw not the heir to a royal throne or ducal residence, but a real child, with its natural petulance, or its delight in toys. He was no doubt influenced by his feelings for his own son.

❛ I have a son of four, who is so beautiful that people look at him in the street in Madrid. He has been so ill that I haven't lived for all the period of his sickness. Thanks be to God he is now better.❜

Letter to Zapater

The little boy in red (4), Don Manuel Osorio Manrique de Zuñiga, plays with a magpie while a cat lies in wait with a gleam in its eye. The son of the Duke of Osuna (3; detail of portrait p. 59), Don Pedro de Alcántara became a painter, member of the Academy of San Fernando and director of the Prado. Francisco de Paula (2), one of the Infantes of Spain, was the favourite son of María Luisa; this was a preparatory sketch for the great painting *The Family of Charles IV*.

In the year 1789 history intervened in Goya's life. On 5 May the States-General met in France: they were to uncover all the evils of old Europe. The first skirmishes of the French Revolution, news of which was not allowed to reach the Spanish people, worried the government and Court in Madrid, who kept themselves fully informed. Within a short while, Louis XVI, completely overtaken by events, sent a desperate secret appeal to his first cousin Charles IV – he had dreamed of taking refuge in Spain since 14 July 1789.

CHAPTER 3
HAZARDS OF FORTUNE

In *The Mannequin* (left), Goya alludes to the political upheavals of the time, the dance of prime ministers in 1792. Right: a *Model of the Bastille* by Lesueur.

Far removed from all this, elated by his recent promotion, Goya painted a series of portraits of Charles IV and María Luisa (most of them quite disappointing). Disturbed by the change of reign and the upheavals in France, the Court lost interest in the decoration of the Royal Palace and the production of tapestry cartoons was halted, which suited Goya. He received fewer commissions from notables, who were probably worried about their income, and realized only one painting, for the altarpiece of the Church of Valdemoro.

Meanwhile Goya's friends and supporters were promoted to high posts. In August 1789 Zapater, who had helped to save Saragossa from shortages, was ennobled in Aragon; on 26 December 1789 Cabarrús, supported by Floridablanca but hated by Lerena, the old finance minister, was made a count. But María Luisa was dangerously hostile to Cabarrús, Jovellanos and Floridablanca: it was soon to become clear that she, not the King, represented the real power.

Martín Zapater was a rich, unmarried businessman, friend and contemporary of Goya. The artist, who painted his portrait in 1790 (left), wrote to Zapater regularly between 1775 and 1799. An essential key to the artist's personality, the letters were unfortunately censored by Zapater's heir, his nephew, who thought them politically too 'free-thinking'.

Ephemeral power: the wheel of fortune turns

A thunderbolt now struck the *ilustrados*: Cabarrús was arrested on 25 June 1790 for no known reason and put in solitary confinement by order of Lerena. Jovellanos, who early in the year had been dispatched 'to see how coal was extracted in Asturias' (in other words, banished), rushed back to Madrid to defend his friend, but to no avail. All doors were closed, and he had no choice but to return to Gijon in despair. His exile lasted seven years. Goya himself was suddenly issued with a permit, on 17 July 1790, to 'go and breathe the sea air' in Valencia.

By October Goya was back in Saragossa, where he painted a portrait of Zapater. On his return to Madrid at Christmas 1790, he found the climate had changed. He

had been ill, and now went anxiously to see Charles IV, who had been told by 'vile men' that Goya 'did not want to serve him'. 'Enough of that subject,' he wrote to Zapater, 'it turns my stomach.'

We now know that the Court Painter Maëlla had advised the powers-that-be of Goya's 'ill-will': he did not want to continue work on the tapestry cartoons. The director of the Factory wrote directly to the King to complain. Lerena intervened and the painter was given an outright order. It was a serious matter, the more so as Goya had lost some of his protectors. Bayeu stepped in and Goya had to yield, not in anger but in fear. On 6 May 1791 he finished the sketch of *The Wedding*, the largest cartoon, for a tapestry to hang in the King's office at the Escorial: a superb work illustrating the marriage of a grotesque old man to a youthful beauty. The King

The subject of *The Wedding* (below) was the three ages of life: children on the left, a married couple and an old man. Interpreted in the socio-political context of the period, however, the painting is in fact mocking marriages in which a girl weds a man the age of her grandfather for his money or title.

The new Royal Palace in Madrid, designed by J.B. Sacchetti, was inspired by Piedmontese baroque. Giaquinto, Mengs and Tiepolo all contributed to the interior decor.

wanted amusing subjects and was given them in plenty; another marvellous example was *The Mannequin*, a cartoon laden with undertones. The same year Goya moved effortlessly from burlesque satire to the charms of childhood, painting a winsome portrait of the little *Luis Cistué*, blond, pink and blue.

In October 1791 Goya went back to Saragossa where he probably painted his portrait of Canon Pignatelli (only a copy survives). In December 1791 he submitted a bill for the seven cartoons he had just finished, the last of his life. In February 1792 he wrote an amusing letter to Zapater describing himself as 'giant Goya', and soon after spoke of drawing up his genealogy, with a view to being ennobled; he insisted on the need to preserve an element of dignity and to give up listening to *seguidillas* (popular tunes) as of yore. He may even have dreamed of seeking an honorary post at Court, like Velázquez, as a way of escaping the manual labour of the artist.

Meanwhile the repercussions of the French Revolution are felt at Court

The arrest of the fleeing French king at Varennes in 1791 made

Spain hostile to any kind of liberalism. Lerena died early in 1792. Much was to change. In February 1792 Floridablanca, who some thought incompetent, others an incumbrance, was dismissed and replaced by the old Count of Aranda, ejected in his turn on November 1792 in favour of the strong, blond Godoy, twenty-five-year-old favourite of the Queen, Duke of Alcudia and virtual commander of the Spanish armies. In August 1792, the King of France now dethroned and imprisoned, Spain feared that the war already declared by the French Republic on the German Empire might reach the Iberian peninsula. In January 1793 Louis XVI was guillotined and France did indeed declare war on Spain.

Although little is known of Goya's life in 1792, or of how, in the space of two years, this admired and respected painter became a virtual outcast, the political disturbance of the Court caused by events in France and the fall of several of his protectors must have disrupted his career.

Queen María Luisa, a passionate intriguer, was the wife of a gallant king with little inclination to govern. She tried to gain power through her favourite, Godoy. He owed his career to her and acted as her unquestioning official mouthpiece, enabling her to rule single-handed. A French diplomat later wrote: 'At the age of fifty the Queen has pretentions and coquetry barely forgivable in a young and pretty woman.' Goya's portrait of her (above) dates from 1789.

In this critical year there is almost no correspondence with Zapater, no royal or private commissions. The only surviving documents are an account from June, relating to the last tapestry cartoons, some bills, the results of genealogical researches in May and July, and the reply to a request for a recommendation in early autumn. There is evidence that he attended the Academy of San Fernando on 2 September, and on 14 October he presented a report there on the teaching of art. Thereafter, total silence.

Goya's professional difficulties are compounded by a worse affliction: illness leaves him deaf

On 17 January 1793 Goya wrote that he had been in bed for two months, and reported that he was now authorized

to visit Seville and Cadiz. Here the mystery deepens: this letter to the treasurer of the Osunas was addressed from Madrid, whereas we know that from 5 January 1793 he was in Cadiz from a letter Zapater wrote to Sebastián Martínez, the rich Cadiz businessman and collector who took Goya in. Martínez reported that the latter arrived in his house seriously ill, having come from Seville. Moreover, in January the high chamberlain of the Court, the Duke of Frias, gave Goya two months' leave 'to go to Andalusia', without specifying dates. He was seized with paralysis, said his friends, in letters full of innuendo. Zapater, who mentioned Goya's 'lack of thought', was probably referring to some rash decision, rather than to the fact that he was believed to have a venereal disease.

The Inquisition was instrumental in the Reconquest and the expulsion of the Jews in Spain, but lost its power in the 18th century, when it was accused of confusing heresy and humanism. However it came to prominence again at the end of the century and in this painting, *Scene from the Inquisition* (1812–14), Goya protests against its sudden revival.

This admirable self-portrait, a tinted drawing in Indian ink, is generally dated 1795–7. Goya portrays himself as a dreamer, almost in the grip of a nightmare.

Why had Goya gone to stay in Andalusia without getting the required official permission first? Was he involved in the unsuccessful attempt to rescue Louis XVI, secretly entrusted to Cabarrús? There are clues, but no firm evidence. The Spanish Bourbons were doing all they could to save their cousin from sentence of death. Goya's grandson later told a fantastic story of a flight over the Sierra Morena, which may contain an element of truth. Meanwhile the powers of the Inquisition had been reinforced to resist the advance of the French Revolution and a climate of suspicion and fear reigned in Madrid.

Well cared-for, Goya recovered the use of his limbs. He still heard loud buzzing noises in his head but his dizziness had gone. The dramatic outcome of his illness

‘I am the same as ever; as far as my health goes, sometimes I feel furious, in that I can hardly put up with my temper, sometimes I feel calmer, as when writing to you now. But I'm already feeling tired; all I can say is that on Monday, God willing, I am going to a bullfight, and I would have liked you to come with me...’

Letter to Zapater

(apparently a type of meningitis) was that he went incurably deaf; a terrible affliction for an outgoing man who loved field sports. He reacted by continuing to work. In summer 1793 he returned to Madrid.

María Rosario de Fernandez, known as 'La Tirana' because her husband, also an actor, played the part of tyrants, was born in Seville in 1775 and died in Madrid in 1803 after a long illness. Famous for her beauty and strict morals, La Tirana moved in cultivated circles.

In early January 1794 new masterpieces emerge from the painter's studio

Irrepressible, Goya reappeared in the capital and sent Bernardo de Yriarte, Vice Protector of the Academy of San Fernando, a series of easel paintings executed on copper illustrating 'national activities'. He had done them 'to occupy my imagination, burdened by the contemplation of my sufferings', to improve his finances, and finally because they were a way of freely expressing his 'invention and caprice' – two key words of his personality. But instead of lamenting his lot, he determined to learn new things and prove to himself and others that he had lost none of his professional skill. Periodically he suffered a relapse, his recovery proving long, but this did not stop him taking up his brush to meet official commissions.

He was asked to paint two well-known military leaders fighting on the Pyrenean front. The first was *General Ricardos* (opposite), who would die at the hands of the enemy early in 1794. This is one of the character portraits at which Goya was to excel; the careful paintwork and brilliant colouring in no way deflected his search for psychological truth. He also painted a portrait of lieutenant-colonel *Felix Colon de Larréategui*, whose brothers were friends of

Cabarrús, and brilliantly transposed onto canvas the disdain written on the man's tight, thin lips, probably finding him antipathetic while still admiring his bearing. Another fine portrait from the same year is that of *Ramón Posado y Soto*, a relation of Jovellanos' brother-in-law, who has left a record in a letter of his visit to Goya and reports his total deafness. In the midst of these ironical and stiff gentlemen there was a friendlier face: that of the actress *La Tirana* (left), a corpulent, full-blown lady first painted by Goya in 1794, when she was bidding her farewells to the stage; as always with a model whom he knows, he portrays her with great naturalness. The impeccable execution shows him in full control of his brush, though it suited him to tell the director of the Factory that serious illness prevented him from working.

General Ricardos was killed on 13 March 1794. His death deprived the Spanish army of one of its best generals, one of whose claims to fame was that in the war against France in 1793 he won the Battle of Truilles in the Roussillon. His widow gave this portrait of him to Godoy.

The year 1794 is crucial for France and Spain

Interestingly, in April, Jovellanos, who for four years had not once in his *Journal* mentioned the name of Cabarrús, his 'special friend' still under house arrest in Madrid, referred to the review of his case. Cabarrús' daughter Teresa, imprisoned in France under the order of Robespierre, who had rightly suspected her of conspiring with Spain, encouraged Jean Tallien and his friends to revolt: but the *coup d'état* of 9 Thermidor (the eleventh month of Republican calendar) succeeded, Robespierre and his men were guillotined, and the Terror decreased, to the immense relief of France and, indeed, the rest of Europe.

The Spanish government ardently wanted the war to end and the Convention to send them the two children of Louis XVI. Teresa Cabarrús, now Tallien's wife, tried to negotiate the release of her father; it was whispered that through Cabarrús she was the secret go-between of Godoy and the French committees.

The atmosphere in the Spanish Court was less tense; Goya profited by gaining new clients, often associates or intimates of his old patrons. The Count of Carpio, President of the Council of Military Orders, part of the Council of the Bank of San Carlos, was a great friend of Jovellanos. His thirty-three-year-old wife, the Marquise of

Solana, from a distinguished Basque family, had her portrait painted by Goya, perhaps as a memento for her only daughter, for she died shortly afterwards.

1795: Goya meets his most famous model, the Duchess of Alba

In July 1795 France, Spain and Prussia signed the Treaty of Basel. The war was over. Honours rained on the heads of the nobility: Godoy became Prince of Peace, Goya was asked to paint the portrait of the Duke of Alba, and then of his wife – the famous full-length picture of her, a symphony of white, red and black on a background of greenish-yellow sierra and blue sky, signed and dated 1795, in which he seems for the first time to place his model in 'real landscape'.

French romantic writers have imagined a tale of passion between the grand lady and the deaf artist. In truth no contemporary document or written evidence offers the slightest proof. Except perhaps a few etchings in *The Caprices.*

Goya must have known the Duchess for a long time. Flighty and whimsical, she mixed happily with commoners, bullfighters, students, even peasants. That he should have fallen in love with her in the relaxed circumstances of their many portrait sittings is perfectly plausible; but, of course,

❛You would have done better to come and help me paint the Alba lady who came into the studio for me to paint her face, and then went off again; I certainly prefer this to painting her on canvas. I am also to do a full-length portrait of her and she's coming back as soon as I've finished a sketch I am now doing of the Duke of Alcudia on horseback.❜

Letter to Zapater

The history of the album referred to as the Sanlúcar Album, which includes this tinted drawing of the Duchess of Alba (left), is far from clear. It is known that the Duchess stayed at Sanlúcar de Barrameda, a port on the Atlantic coast in Andalusia, in 1796–7, and that Goya was there between May and July 1796, but the reasons for the journey remain obscure. The album contains eighteen sketches in which the Duchess appears two or three times; some are reworked in *The Caprices.*

A remarkable woman, the Marquise of Solana (below) was highly charitable; she maintained an orphanage, and it was she who was delegated to lecture the Duchess of Alba (left) on her behaviour.

The transparent blue-grey background of the Marquise's portrait, the light gauze of the shawl, the pink bow in the hair, are handled in a wholly illusionistic manner. Transcending her homely features, Goya captures the intangible, brave and generous spirit of the Marquise. One feels that he admired this courageous woman who, knowing that she was going to die, stands fragile and indomitable, a worthy symbol of Spanish pride.

he was stone-deaf and fifty, while the beautiful Duchess was only thirty-five. She may simply have been amusing herself with a harmless artist, little suspecting that with the pitiless point of his etching needle in *The Caprices*, in a few trenchant drawings and three confessional paintings, he would render her immortal – and perhaps not always in a way she would have liked. Humour is more apparent than any notion of love in his little canvas of the Duchess and her chaperone (right), dated 1795.

Bayeu died in July 1795; Goya, who bore no grudge, exhibited his portrait (below) at the Academy, unfinished, but remarkable in its psychological acuity. The range of greys and whites is skilfully applied in transparent scumbling. Goya sought through Godoy's influence with the King to get the post of First Court Painter; but he refused. Yriarte, interceding with the responsible official, was no more successful. Goya was, however, elected Director of Painting at the Academy of San Fernando in September, at a salary of 4000 reals.

In November 1795 Cabarrús was at last pardoned and rehabilitated, through Godoy's influence; the former banker was, in truth, a good financial adviser who helped the Prince of Peace with his investments. Cabarrús, an incorrigible optimist, was undaunted: he would not rest till his 'enlightened' friends came to power and did not see that times had changed.

On 4 January 1796 the Court went to Andalusia to venerate the remains of Saint Ferdinand in Seville. The Duke of Alba was with the royal party. In May, Goya too was in Andalusia, in Sanlúcar de Barrameda, where the Albas owned a palace. On 9 June, the Duke died in Seville and was buried there.

According to the *Journal* of the poet Moratín, who returned to Spain at the end of 1796, Goya, again ill, was then in Cadiz. It was probably in 1796 that he painted his

A sign of the changing social climate, Goya, Court Painter, portrayed the Duchess of Alba, the grandest lady in Spain after the queen, in an intimate scene: *The Duchess of Alba and her Chaperone* (right). The painting resembles one of Hogarth's satirical works. In her will the Duchess left Goya and his son, in common with a number of other faithful servants, an income of ten reals a day.

Francisco Bayeu (left), Goya's brother-in-law, was born in Saragossa in 1734. Ambitious, an excellent craftsman, he had done work for the churches of Saragossa before being noticed by the painter Mengs, who summoned him to Madrid to participate in the decoration of the Royal Palace. A tremendous worker, but also finicky, never satisfied, ever recriminating, claiming his due, niggling when he thought the terms offered him inadequate, Bayeu had mostly worked on frescos. He had considerable family responsibilities, having brought up two brothers, Ramón and Manuel, who were also painters, and two sisters, including Josefa, Goya's wife; on his death he left a large fortune.

three great canvases for the oratory of Santa Cueva in Cadiz; in their bold layout, original technique and exquisite colouring, they breathe new spirit into the traditional iconography of the life of Christ.

Goya's drawings for the so-called Sanlúcar albums are among his first real studies from life. In them he communicated his ideas and preoccupations, locked as he was in deafness. The Duchess of Alba was featured two or three times, as well as a strikingly pretty young woman, naked or barely dressed, of unknown identity.

Goya painted the Duchess in a second masterly portrait dated 1797, bearing the inscription in the sand '*Solo Goya*' ('Only Goya'); she is dressed as a *maja*, in mantilla and black skirt, against a luminous coastal landscape. Her arched figure, her proud bearing – albeit tinged with vulgarity – and her sad expression show that Goya, lucid as ever, knew how to reveal the unconscious theatricality of his illustrious model – so skilfully, perhaps, that one at first fails to appreciate it. In the spring of 1797 Goya quit his post as Director of the Academy of San Fernando on health grounds. He began work on his great series of etchings, *The Caprices*.

In Paris, the government of the Directoire was troubling Godoy, who refused to meet all its demands. To compound matters his passion for the pretty Pepita Tudo, whom he probably met on a trip with the Royal Family in Andalusia, complicated his relations with the Queen,

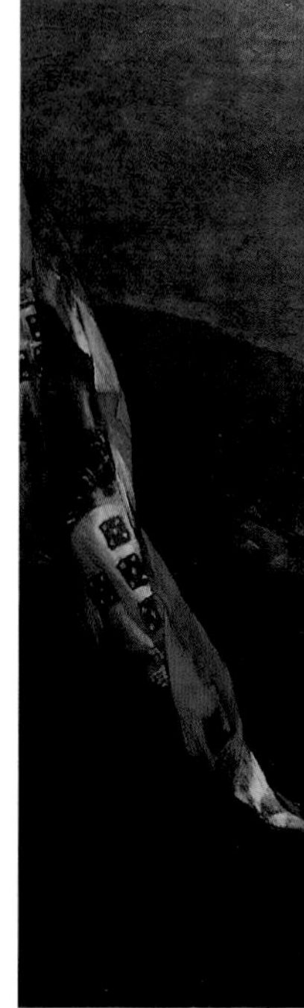

Jovellanos (below right), Goya's friend and protector, is here portrayed with great natural simplicity. He is impeccably elegant in an exquisite silk dress coat. Goya achieves perfect accord between the model's features and the feelings and thoughts he conveys; the high forehead expressive of great intelligence, the eyes looking directly at the artist, with great candour, melancholy, and also doubt. Left: *Self-portrait*, the frontispiece for *The Caprices*.

who forced him in 1797 to marry the Countess of Chinchón, daughter of Don Luis and cousin of Charles IV.

Caught in a web of intrigue, Godoy looked to the liberals for support and, on the advice of Cabarrús, brought friends of his into the government: Jovellanos into the Ministry of Justice, Bernardo de Yriarte into Agriculture and Francisco Saavedra into Finance. Goya was naturally commissioned to paint their portraits, between 1797 and 1798.

He represents Yriarte, ceremonious, utterly sure of himself in a powdered wig; Jovellanos, distinguished, a dreamer weighed down by

Manuel Godoy, born in Badajoz in 1767, joined the royal bodyguard in 1784, when the Infanta María Luisa noticed him. From 1789, when she became queen, she openly displayed her feelings for him. Godoy rose to the highest military posts, becoming Prime Minister in November 1792, and Prince of Peace in 1795. In 1808, when the Napoleonic troops invaded, he just escaped assassination. He died in Paris in 1852. Goya painted this portrait (above) in 1801.

cares, a hint of benevolence, nonetheless, in his eyes (an indication of his feeling for the artist).

France under the Directoire secretly demanded the dismissal of Godoy, who was accused of supporting England. On 28 March 1798 he fell; his newly installed liberal government disintegrated during the following summer.

In the spring of 1798, by order of María Luisa, Goya is asked to decorate the Royal Chapel of San Antonio de la Florida in Madrid

Goya was fifty-two, completely deaf, in failing health; yet he did not hesitate to climb the scaffolding to paint another dome, the most famous of the modern age. Free of the nit-picking Bayeu and the grumpy canons, Goya could at last work as he liked.

He represented a popular scene unfolding round the drum of the dome as if it were quite natural for Saint Anthony to preach ten metres above ground. A symphony in grey and blue, dashed with yellow, the fresco astonishes in its inventiveness, its expressive freedom. The work took Goya some four months (from

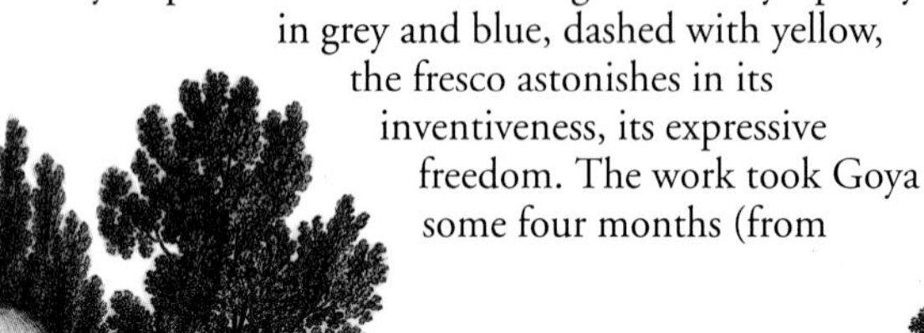

From the 17th century, the shrine of Saint Anthony of Padua stood in the grounds of La Florida, below the park of the Royal Palace. Wanting to extend the royal grounds, Charles IV and María Luisa bought the adjacent land and decided to build a new chapel, San Antonio de la Florida (interior above).

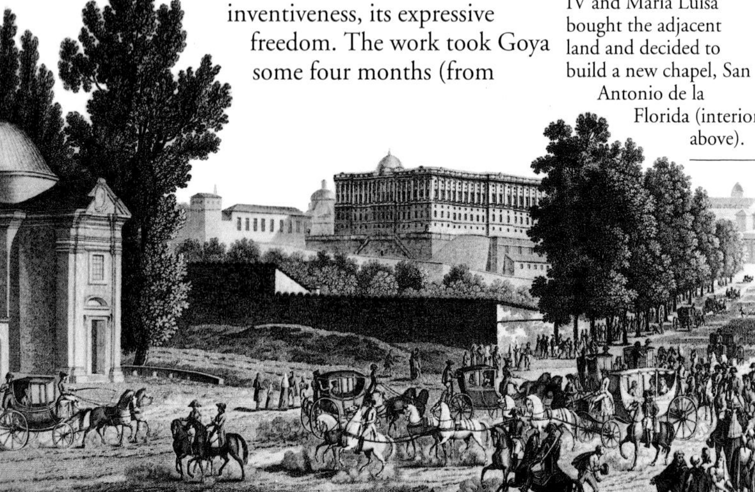

August to the end of November). He sketched the composition directly onto fresh plaster, modifying the original drawing as he went along with masterly skill. The angels on the pendentives seem to have emerged from the studio of Renoir, so far are they in advance of their time.

In June 1798 Goya delivered six little paintings to the Duke and Duchess of Osuna for the Alameda. These scenes look ahead to *The Caprices.* The large he-goat in *The Witches' Sabbath,* for example, was a popular devil in Aragon, a leitmotiv in Goya's work after his period of crisis. Having achieved full technical mastery, he transferred his dreams and obsessions onto canvas, as if capturing cinematically what passed through his head, his hand following his imagination with only a second's delay.

Goya was astonishingly productive. Early in 1799 he submitted *The Arrest of Christ* to Toledo Cathedral for the sacristy. The nocturnal light is so perfectly observed that to look at it is almost to participate in Christ's drama – Goya has evoked the 'magic of atmosphere' that pervades amidst the cries and shouts.

Thanks to Goya the little hermitage of San Antonio de la Florida has become one of the artistic shrines of Madrid. In his fresco (detail above) the monotony of the circular balustrade is suddenly broken by the white patch of a great processional cloth accompanying the litany of the faithful. The figure on the left suggests the sibyls of Michelangelo, who had a strong influence on Goya's frescos.

The publication of *The Caprices* is announced on 6 and 19 February 1799: they can be bought from a perfumer at Goya's address

The perfumer later reported that *The Caprices* were withdrawn from sale after two days; because of the Inquisition, only twenty-seven copies were sold, four to the Duke and Duchess of Osuna.

The work was considered to be too free-thinking, too inflammatory, to be allowed to fall into the hands of just anybody – even if it was incomprehensible to the uninitiated. Pitiless satires on social behaviour, which also touched on Court scandals, some plates were conceived as puzzles, and must be solved within their historical context.

It is the nature of great works to communicate at a universal level in exposing the flaws of society. Goya's talent as an etcher was so rare, so original, his imagination so vigorous, his technique so skilled, that in giving artistic expression to the social criticisms formulated by his friends he invested them with momentous significance. His subjects included prostitution, superstition, the Inquisition, unbridled ambition, the venality and abuse of power. His ideas were always transformed into tremendously vital images.

It is possible that the French ambassador Ferdinand Guillemardet hid a copy of *The Caprices* in the Embassy. Goya painted a magnificent portrait (far right) of this ad hoc diplomat, who was originally a doctor from Burgundy. The painting was exhibited in 1799 at the Academy of San Fernando. Guillemardet fell in love with the Marquise of Santa Cruz, the young aunt by marriage of the Duchess of Alba, and closely linked to Goya. The *Portrait in a Mantilla* (right), probably painted in 1799, is a marvellous work in which Goya gives free rein to his imagination while achieving a perfect likeness. These two portraits now hang opposite each other in the Louvre.

In *The Caprices* one finds illustrations of proverbs, more-or-less direct criticisms of society, witticisms on witches – all ranging in tone from mockery to anger. Here *The Sleep of Reason Produces Monsters.*

The Marquise of Santa Cruz (right), née Mariana Waldstein, offspring of a great Austrian family, was the second wife of the Marquis of Santa Cruz. An intriguing tale alludes to a young Marquise of S. with whom Goya was in love, the wife of an old chamberlain. This painting could be her portrait.

Ferdinand Guillemardet (1765–1809) was a member of the National Convention. Having voted for the death of Louis XVI, he was one of the legal witnesses for the birth of Eugène Delacroix whose father, Charles Delacroix, was Minister for Foreign Affairs. The latter appointed him ambassador to Madrid, why we do not know, since Guillemardet's speciality was the organization of military hospitals. He is said to have died mad. Goya did the above portrait of him in 1798.

The significance of *The Caprices* either escaped the Royal Family or they brushed it aside. In September 1799 Queen María Luisa commissioned a new portrait from Goya, who painted her in a mantilla. She was most satisficd with it and on 9 October announced that the artist had next done a portrait of her on horseback in three sittings, that he had been very demanding about her pose, and that all was a good likeness, both of herself and the horse Marcial.

CHAPTER 4
COURT PAINTER

Goya, admitted to the corridors of power, observed the decadence of the Spanish monarchy. While he seems to glorify the Royal Family in his paintings (portrait of María Luisa, left), his etchings (right, from *The Caprices*) can be sharply critical.

Su ancho 10 pies y 14 dedos. Su precio

The delighted Queen wrote to Godoy: ‘It’s said to be a better likeness than the portrait in the mantilla.’ The vast canvas was indeed one of Goya’s triumphs. With a view of the Sierra de Guadarrama worthy of Velázquez, it had great naturalness and realism. Head held back, María Luisa looks out with an air of amused defiance, colluding, benevolent, revealing much of a personality that has been variously judged by posterity.

‘I can’t enjoy myself if I cannot see other people. Don’t delay ...and don’t forget my glasses... I can’t see anything.’
Letter to Zapater, 1792

In France came 18 Brumaire (the second month of the Republican calendar) 1799, Bonaparte’s *coup d’état.* His sights were set on the Imperial throne, and despotism gradually spread over Europe.

In Madrid the government, Godoy above all, quickly submitted to him. The *ilustrados* were exiled, particularly as Cabarrús and his daughter Teresa Tallien, now the mistress of the banker Gabriel Julien Ouvrard, represented financial interests opposed to those of Bonaparte, and were ruthlessly cast aside.

Goya, while retaining his clear realistic vision of the world around him, broke free from political and ideological groups: he had learned prudence and did not wish to lose what had cost him so much to obtain.

Goya’s self-portraits (the above was painted around 1800) suggest an element of self-examination.

On 31 October 1799 he was at last appointed First Court Painter, at an annual salary of 50,000 reals; he informed Zapater of his promotion and added without the slightest modesty: 'The royals are mad about me.'

In 1799 he painted the prestigious full-length portrait of the actress La Tirana dressed in the style of the Directoire, in an antique dress adorned with a eye-catching scarf of pink satin spangled with gold. The work has the relaxed air characteristic of Goya's portraits of friends. Another example is his *Portrait of Moratín* (right), painted on 16 July 1799 with startling psychological acuteness; it was in Moratín's company that Goya looked for an apartment in January 1800. The house he had occupied since 1778 had been bought by Godoy for his mistress Pepita Tudo and he had to move. In June 1800 the painter bought, for the considerable sum of 234,000 reals, a property at 15 Calle Valverde, off the Calle del Desengaño. Goya was now a householder.

Moratín (below) was a poet and playwright. His sparkling style is as evocative as Goya's drawings.

As Court Painter, Goya turns his hand as readily to courtesans, princesses, ministers and kings

Goya of course knew Pepita Tudo, the supposed model for *Nude Maja*, a painting that had been noticed by art lovers in a drawing room of Godoy's palace in November 1800. The nude was not frequently represented in Spanish art, so Goya's canvas was a rarity. The superb figure of the *Maja* seems sculpted in white wax, strangely erotic in its immobility.

On 22 April 1800 María Luisa wrote to tell Godoy that Goya was busy painting his wife the Countess of Chinchón (far right). It was his best female portrait, with that of *La Solana*, and conveys great intimacy despite the reserved attitude of the model. It is apparent that Goya preferred the charming princess to the provocative Pepita. The silvery muslin dress stands out against a plain background and the gentle face framed in a frizz of fair hair is adorned with ears of wheat, symbol of forthcoming motherhood.

The Princess of Peace soon had her fill of her husband's licentious behaviour. Taking refuge in silent contempt,

Probably a portrait of Godoy's mistress, Pepita Tudo, not of the Duchess of Alba as often supposed, the *Nude Maja* (above) adorned a wall in the Prime Minister's palace, next to another famous nude by Velázquez, *Venus at her Mirror* (*The Rokeby Venus*, 1650–1). When Godoy fell, the painting was hidden in a backroom of the Academy of San Fernando until 1900. In 1901 it was taken to the Prado with the *Clothed Maja.*

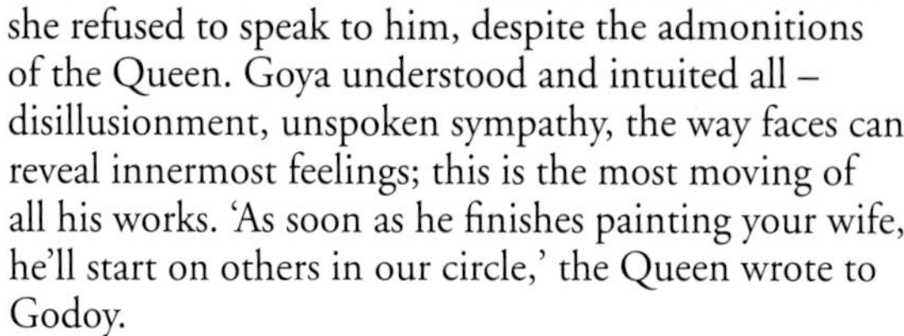

she refused to speak to him, despite the admonitions of the Queen. Goya understood and intuited all – disillusionment, unspoken sympathy, the way faces can reveal innermost feelings; this is the most moving of all his works. 'As soon as he finishes painting your wife, he'll start on others in our circle,' the Queen wrote to Godoy.

The sketches of portraits for *The Family of Charles IV* were ready by August 1800. Knowing the speed at which Goya worked, the painting itself was probably finished in the next few months.

The Royal Family were shown life-size, standing grouped in front of a drawing-room wall in the palace, the King and Queen in the foreground. Goya is seen in the shadows on the left, more modestly than Velázquez in *Las Meninas*.

He also executed two full-length portraits of the King and Queen (in a turban), the best of the series, and an equestrian portrait of Charles IV, which was less successful than that of María Luisa; the series was finished in June 1801.

Godoy's wife, the Countess of Chinchón (above), had already been painted by Goya as a child in 1783 amidst her family (*Family of the Infante Don Luis*, pp. 42–3). Jovellanos, invited to lunch by Godoy at the end of 1797, was indignant to see the Prime Minister at table with his wife, the Princess of Peace, on his right, and his mistress, Pepita Tudo, on his left. 'There is no solution', wrote Jovellanos sorrowfully, in a cry that anticipates the one inscribed by Goya beneath one of *The Caprices*.

In *The Family of Charles IV* Goya marries the psychological truth of his figures to a powerful magic aura. One might indeed get the wrong impression from this picture of the monarchs. According to outside reports, the ugliness of the Queen matched the absurdity of her costumes and the worthy Charles IV was no more conspicuous for his intelligence than was his sister. The Prince of Parma (detail above) was, however, better endowed. The upper detail shows the Infanta María Josefa.

Fresh disturbances at Court: at the end of 1800 Godoy regains political control, while Lucien Bonaparte is sent to Madrid as French ambassador

In May 1801 the King and Queen undertook an expedition to Portugal: the War of the Oranges. It won Godoy laurels, not wholly deserved, but nonetheless an occasion to be painted by Goya in the nonchalant attitude of a victorious general (see p. 77). The portrait is somewhat disappointing as Godoy seems to escape the artist's psychological eye, unless the latter had simply lost interest in his sitter.

Goya did further work for Godoy between 1801 and 1803, four *tondos* illustrating business occupations to decorate his palace. Also from this period is the *Clothed Maja*, probably another picture of Godoy's mistress.

In July 1802 the Duchess of Alba died at the age of forty, not poisoned, as was rumoured, but after a month's illness. There survives a tinted drawing by Goya of a projected tomb for the Duchess. In a few strokes he movingly evokes the little face and the closed eyes of his patroness.

In July 1803 the painter gave the King the copper plates of *The Caprices* for his engraving studio and the unsold prints, in return for help with his son Javier's travels. This was to be Goya's last contact with the Court until 1808, though he continued to collect his wages.

The figure of *Industry* is admirably integrated into the circular form of a *tondo.* Goya plays with the theme of the circle, featuring wheels and arched windows, and lights the scene from behind.

Neither his private nor public life seemed to suffer any consequences. In addition to a comfortable salary he had, thanks to his work, built up a respectable capital over the years and in 1803 bought another house in the Calle de los Reyes in Madrid. Zapater died that same year, 1803. One wonders why the correspondence between the two men ceased after 1799. Did the Aragonese businessman come to live in Madrid, as Goya had often begged him to do, or could it be that they had they quarrelled? There is no documentary evidence to support either theory.

The Count of Fernán Núñez (below), Spanish ambassador to France, was a patron of the arts and member of the Academy of San Fernando in 1804. At the election of a new director of the Academy he voted for Goya with eight other academicians; twenty-nine supported a minor artist, Gregorio Ferro. Núñez thus gave proof of his good taste and showed his appreciation of the artist who had just painted his portrait.

Until 1808, in the years before the War of Independence broke out, Goya concentrates almost exclusively on portraits

In 1803–4 he painted two of his best portraits of young men. The first was the twenty-four-year-old *Count of Fernán Núñez*, son of a close friend of Charles III. His tall, strong figure, wrapped in a traditional black cape, stands out against a magnificent background, a splendid two-pointed hat crowning his handsome dark head in the manner of a Velázquez. Here Goya shows himself full master of his talent, perfectly marrying stylization and realism.

From now on it is hard to escape the rakish pose in Goya's work, the seductive countenance of the typical Spanish male, the *majo*. In 1804 Goya was asked to paint the *Marquis of San Adrián*, a friend of Cabarrús and a refined and cultivated man from a noble family of Navarre.

The full-length portrait displays an English influence in the model's crossed legs, a stance rare among the more ceremonious Spaniards. It is a magnificent work, the artist paying great attention to the workmanship, colouring, and rendering of the open, sympathetic expression of the young face. In the same period Goya painted two charming children, Clara de Soria and her little brother.

Goya stayed true to his first patrons, who amply rewarded him. Members of the Alba family continued to sit for him, among them the *Marquise of Villafranca* (right) who, armed with brush and palette, is busy painting her husband. Her full countenance, lacking real beauty, glows with vitality.

In 1805 a number of fine-looking women were immortalized by Goya's brush: *Isabel de Lobo y Porcel* (above) wears an elegant version of the native dress of Andalusia, a tall beribboned comb supporting a black mantilla. Her huge doe eyes, proud yet tender, her sensual mouth, perfect features and faultless bust make her one of the most beautiful women in the history of art.

Joaquina, second daughter of the Osunas, who were among Goya's first patrons, married the son of the Marquis of Santa Cruz. The artist portrays her stretched out on a couch like Madame Récamier, a chaste and graceful muse. The painting recalls that of the *Nude Maja* in its smooth, firm rendering of youthful flesh, typical of the visual plasticity of the female form in Goya's work; the handling of the cloth on the other hand is strikingly free.

Isabel de Lobo y Porcel had married Antonio Porcel in 1802; he was a member of the council of Castille and a great friend of Goya, who painted her portrait (detail left).

Tomasa Palafox (right), Marquise of Villafranca and cousin of the famous General Palafox, hero of Saragossa, was sister-in-law by marriage of the Duchess of Alba, whose deathbed she attended. It is through her we know that the Duchess was not poisoned, contrary to the rumours circulating at the time.

In 1805 Goya's son Javier was twenty-one. The best-looking little boy in Madrid – in the eyes of his father – was now an elegant young man, rich, spoilt, something of a dandy. Calling himself a painter, he had not progressed beyond a few daubs.

Notwithstanding the banishment and forced departure of the former directors of the Bank of San Carlos, Goya had kept in contact with the worlds of business and finance. He arranged the marriage of his son to Gumersinda Goicoechea (a distant relation of the Goicoechea in Saragossa), whose maternal uncle was Leon Galarza, director of the Bank of San Carlos. Goya's son could thus live on his private income.

Goya's abiding philosophy: never underestimate the importance of money

He knew that artistic freedom depended on financial independence: that alone enabled him to express himself as he wished, not as others wished. His private wealth, accumulated by work, and his business contacts allowed him to survive political crises. These contacts also gave him a broader view of life than was found in the limited world of the Court.

His son's marriage occasioned two outstanding portraits: the bridegroom, a figure in grey, is observed with tenderness and realism, a pictorial *tour de force*; the exquisite young bride could in her costume have stepped out of an Indian miniature. The couple lived with Goya at first, before moving to the house he gave them in the Calle de los Reyes.

It was at this house, in 1806, that Mariano was born, the eighth wonder of the

The subject of this painting (right) was inspired by popular 19th-century engravings known as *alleluya*, a type of comic strip. It shows a monk, Pedro de Zaldivia, being attacked by the bandit Pedro Piñero, known as 'El Maragato' (a waggoner in the Léon region). The brave and determined monk succeeded in disarming the bandit and bringing about his arrest. The modernity of the compositions (this is one of a series of six) is striking: they succeed each other like scenes in a film. The figures are shown in close-up, their attitudes marking the progression of events and the reversal of the situation. The colours are fresh and clear, the workmanship quick and purposeful; each brushstroke makes a point. Although Goya is not a painter of movement, he is a painter of violence and force, and the figures here do seem to move with tremendous power.

❛As far as I'm concerned, all I can say is that I always work with the same seriousness on whatever I want, without having to accommodate any enemy, without being subject to anyone: I don't want to dance attendance on anyone.❜

Letter to Zapater

world in the eyes of his grandfather, who happily recorded his ecstatic delight. Goya was then sixty but responded to life as if the years had taken no toll.

The growing middle classes were the mainstay of his custom: *Porcel*, husband of the lovely Lobo, painted with his game dog; *Felix de Azara*, the naturalist; the *Suredas* (he was director of the Buen Retiro porcelain factory); *Sabasa García*, a marvellous female portrait, poetic, mysterious; the superb portrait of María Mazon entitled *The Bookshop in the Calle de Carretas*; *Pedro Mocarte* looking like a retired bullfighter; all of them presented in terms of their individual personality and style, with a breathtaking range of attitudes, expressions and colours.

In 1806 the bandit El Maragato was arrested, an event which but for Goya would have sunk into oblivion. The artist illustrated the drama in six episodes, choosing his 'scoop' for maximum impact in the manner of a 20th-century reporter. Yet another facet of his talent is revealed.

For his son's marriage Goya made a series of drawings. Below: Javier. Left: Gumersinda.

On 21 October 1805 at Trafalgar, Spain, ally of France, lost its armada, one of the finest in the world. French bankers financially involved in Spain, Récamier and Ouvrard at their head, suffered spectacular bankruptcies, and the Emperor Napoleon thus brought about the ruin of the Spanish treasury. To compound matters he was determined to rid Europe of the last reigning Bourbons and instal his brother Joseph on the Spanish throne.

CHAPTER 5
INTO THE DARK

A terror-struck populace flees as *The Colossus* (left) turns his back: Goya could be alluding to Godoy, who unleashed violence and turned his back on the victims. The etching (right) is from *The Disasters of War.*

Despite the French victories of 1807, money was running short. The English tightened the noose and Napoleon decided to invade Spain. His schemes were aided by the weakness of Godoy and the divisions in the Spanish monarchy: Crown Prince Ferdinand, dim-witted and ill-advised, was foolish enough to seek the Emperor's help in deposing his father Charles IV and driving out the Prince of Peace.

The Spanish people, as usual, knew little of the political upheavals; but so hated was Godoy that Napoleon was seen as a saviour. When the French invaded in December 1807 they were at first well received. However, when in March 1808 Joachim Murat was appointed the Emperor's lieutenant-general in Spain and crossed the Pyrenees to take command of the French army, deployed from Old Castille to Catalonia, the Court in Madrid took fright. On 18 March there was a revolt at the Aranjuez Palace. Godoy narrowly escaped assassination by Prince Ferdinand's supporters, and fled to France. Charles IV abdicated in favour of his son

This engraving illustrates the short-lived triumph, at the end of March 1808, of the new king Ferdinand VII who was welcomed in Madrid like a saviour. It also explains the despair the people felt when they learned, a month later, that their sovereign was imprisoned in Bayonne.

Ferdinand VII and on 23 March the gullible crowds in Madrid, impatiently awaiting the new king, greeted Murat with transports of delight. Charles IV and María Luisa were taken to Bayonne, shortly followed by Ferdinand VII, who had hastened to the Spanish frontier to thank Napoleon. The trap closed. Before the young king departed Goya had been asked by the Academy of San Fernando to paint his portrait (below), on 6 April at 2.30 p.m. The sitting was cut short, never to be resumed, and Goya had to finish the work from memory.

Goya did this full-length painting of Ferdinand VII in 1815. Despite his antipathy to the King, the artist created superb portraits of him.

At the end of April 1808 the Spanish people at last realize that Napoleon has come not to liberate but to conquer

The people were enraged to hear that the last Bourbons had been forced to leave Madrid for Bayonne, where from now on the Emperor held the whole Royal Family captive.

On 2 May violent protests erupted in Madrid. On 3 May they were cruelly repressed by Murat (see pp. 1–7). Six years later Goya immortalized these dates in his paintings *The Second of May, 1808* and *The Third of May, 1808*.

On 15 June the terrible siege of Saragossa began, from which the French first retreated in August. The patriotism of the Aragonese was sustained by General

This painting (1808–10) is entitled *Shootings in a Military Encampment.* The guerillas would readily shoot not only enemy soldiers but also anyone suspected of siding with them. Goya's intensely distressing portrayal of violence in action here is rare; he more usually captured the instant in which it was about to occur.

Palafox, who summoned Goya to Saragossa 'to see and examine the ruins of the city so as to paint the heroic deeds of its inhabitants'. The next French assault, in December, apparently put a stop to the plan.

For six years Spain struggles amid political and military confusion

The vast majority of the Spanish people were fiercely patriotic and waged merciless guerilla warfare against the invader. The loyalties of the aristocrats and liberals were more confused. Some (Floridablanca, Jovellanos, Saavedra) opted for the nationalist government of the Central Junta. Others (Moratín, Yriarte, Cabarrús) rallied

> ❛Every Spaniard now regarded every Frenchman as an enemy. All Spain was armed against France. In the South it was the Cortes who were masters and who governed, calmly, in the normal way in the name of Joseph [Bonaparte]. The North had no firm government; although not wholly free from Joseph, it was under the total sway of guerillas, the bands of Mina, of El Pastor, of the shepherds of La Mesta and the celebrated Empecinada. When a Frenchman fell into the hands of one of these troops they cut him in two or even roasted him alive. The French themselves were hardly less ferocious.❜
>
> Adèle Hugo
> *Victor Hugo related by Victor Hugo*

round the Emperor's brother Joseph. They were called the *afrancesados* ('The Frenchified'). Goya, on the threshold of old age, was no doubt troubled by the divisions among his patrons, but from 1810 he took the side of the patriots on moral grounds.

In these years of warfare, with the advances and retreats of the English, Spanish and French armies bringing death and famine daily in their wake, Goya drew on his resources to produce a series of large canvases which established his reputation as a genre painter: *Majas on a Balcony*, *Young Women* or *The Letter*, *Old Women* or *Que Tal?* ('*How Are You?*'), *The Forge*, *Lazarillo de Tormes*, all a hundred years ahead of their time in style and technique.

Young Women or *The Letter* (opposite), and *Old Women* or *Que Tal?* ('*How Are You?*', left), like Goya's other genre paintings between 1808 and 1812, showed a tendency towards monochrome and a more extensive use of deep, brilliant blacks, contrasting with warm ochres, rough blues, dull greens and, here and there, strident reds; the shadows on the faces are often rendered with black scumbling; the thick paint is applied with a palette knife to create striking relief, and multicoloured spatterings, not taught in any studio, achieve astonishing optical effects. *Old Women*, inquiring of their mirror 'How are you?', could be satirically aimed at María Luisa: one of them has in her hair the famous diamond arrow worn by the Queen in *The Family of Charles IV* (pp. 88–9), suggesting that the painting must have been done after 1808, when the whole of Spain laid the blame for defeat on Godoy and the Queen.

In 1810, horrified and obsessed by the disasters of war, Goya takes up his engraving needles and produces a series of aquatints

Goya's *Disasters of War*, befitting the epic poems of Antiquity, are an overpowering exposition of the horrors of war and the suffering inflicted on the often innocent victims. It is the anguish of the individual rather than of the group that particularly stirred Goya. A man of feeling, he did not passively suffer but used his talent to protest, the violence of his indignation finding expression in the violence of his art.

In picture after picture he returned to the same themes, his use of chiaroscuro and power of pathos inviting comparison with Rembrandt. Only two works, technically very accomplished, concentrate on the military aspect of the struggle: *Making Gunpowder in the Sierra Tardiente* (Aragon) and *Making Bullets.*

In *Making Bullets* (right) and *Making Gunpowder* (below right) Goya pursues his function of 'war-reporter'. In a symphony of deep greens and pale ochres, the figures themselves are incisively represented, their movements captured in an instant of time.

❛They are only hanged men, heaps of dead bodies that get stripped, women that get raped, prisoners that get shot, convents that get robbed, populations that flee, families reduced to begging, patriots that get strangled... But what fine precision, what a profound knowledge of anatomy in all the groups, which seemed to have sprung up by chance at the whim of the etching needle.❜

Théophile Gautier
Wanderings in Spain

Secular evils: the madhouse and the plague hospital

To Goya prison and hospital were both embodiments of the loss of liberty. The biggest lunatic asylum in the whole of Spain was to be found in Saragossa; Goya's friend the poet and magistrate Meléndez Valdés had tried to introduce reforms governing the operation of the hospitals, the intention being to secularize them; but he ran into opposition from the Church which had had control of the institutions until that point, although not running them in an efficient manner. The architectural framework of *The Plague Hospital* (left) is comparable to that seen in *The Madhouse*, painted at the same period, with a highly effective use of back-lighting. The attitudes of the wretched plague victims are, as always in Goya's work, observed with a mixture of realism and deep emotion, a profound pity stripped of all sentimentality.

Secular evils: violence and brigandage

These two little paintings are generally thought to be illustrating scenes of brigandage, but they more probably feature the rape and pillage that were the horrendous consequences of the war. *Brigands Stripping a Woman* (left) shows the degree of perfection Goya reached in his portrayal of the female nude: despite the small format of the canvas, it has an almost antique character. In this canvas, as in *Brigands Shooting their Prisoners* (opposite), the layout, the quality of the light and shade and the harmony of colour recall Rembrandt, the master whom, with Velázquez, Goya most admired.

Goya also attacked the Inquisition and later painted the carnival scene *The Burial of the Sardine* full of political undertones.

In June 1812 Goya's wife Josefa died at the age of sixty-five. An inventory was made of her property, divided between her husband and son; it is a highly interesting document, our only information on the artist's domestic life since correspondence with Zapater ceased. Goya's fortune was now estimated at 360,000 reals.

The year 1812 marks the start of the decline of the power of Napoleon, stuck on the Russian steppes. In Spain Wellington wins victory after victory and enters Madrid in August 1812

Goya was commissioned to paint the Duke of Wellington, who came to the Calle Valverde to pose. Their mutual antipathy was such that the portrait of the English general is close to caricature, with heavy jaw and expressionless eyes. A fierce altercation is said to have ensued between the artist, satisfied with his work, and his illustrious model, outraged by it.

In 1812 the Cortes (the Spanish parliament) reassembled and an ultra-liberal, even daring, constitution was drawn up. The Cortes established itself in Madrid in 1813–4 after the departure of King Joseph and the French army. Goya now painted the *Allegory of the Constitution of 1812*, a spontaneous avowal of his political beliefs and ideals, which were shared by the liberals. They all hoped for the restoration of the monarchy in constitutional form, whereas Ferdinand VII, freed by Napoleon, dreamed only of installing the most autocratic of regimes. In celebration of Spanish patriotism the Cortes organized a competition for painters to immortalize the uprising of 2 May 1808. On 24 February 1814 Goya wrote to the Regency Council presided over by the Cardinal of Bourbon, son of the Infante Don Luis, proposing 'to commemorate with my paintbrush the most notable and heroic actions of our glorious rebellion against the tyrant of Europe'. The offer was accepted on 9 March 1814 and Goya painted his famous scenes of 2 and 3 May 1808 for

Wellington (above) waged war against the Napoleonic troops for four years, finally defeating them at Vitoria on 21 June 1813.

The carnival held on Ash Wednesday in Madrid ended in a burlesque procession followed by a gigantic mannequin carried aloft, attached to it a tiny sardine which the surging crowd took to the banks of the Manzanares for burial. Goya only loosely followed his original in *The Burial of the Sardine*: the sardine is invisible, the mannequin is replaced by a banner decorated with a mask. In fact the picture is closer to a burlesque allegory of the departure of the French army in March 1813.

the remembrance ceremonies held in Madrid on 2 May 1814, which united the whole of Spain in a spirit of national fervour. Like Picasso in *Guernica,* Goya avoids the narrative style. Driven by a sort of mystic force, a steely resolve to avenge the victims of war crimes, he sought by means of his brush to make audible oppressed humanity's cry of revolt, giving universal significance to an episode that without him would never have had the same resonance.

On 13 May 1814 Ferdinand VII, having abolished the 1812 constitution, solemnly enters Madrid, dissolves the Cortes and imprisons the liberal representatives

Dictatorship, obscurantism, proscription – nothing had changed: 'divine reason' was indeed dead. Goya's masterpieces were hastily hidden in the Academy of San Fernando, where they remained, unknown, until the King's death in 1833. But Spain was ruined and Ferdinand VII short of money. He needed the help of the financial circles with which Goya had close links. Following a long inquiry on the attitude of members of the royal household during the French occupation, Goya was cleared of all suspicion of collaboration: he had not even received his salary. Ferdinand VII remained hostile to the artist, but nonetheless left him to work in peace. The best picture of the period is the *Portrait of General Palafox on Horseback* (hero of the siege of Saragossa).

In this self-portrait (left), given by his son to the Academy of San Fernando, Goya seems somehow appeased, less tormented than in his self-portraits painted between 1794 and 1800. It is a relaxed view of himself: his collar is unbuttoned, and while his expression is serious he seems less self-critical. Perhaps this is because he was in love with Leocadia Weiss, a young relative of his daughter-in-law.

On 30 March 1815 the Company of the Philippines (founded by Cabarrús) held a general assembly presided over, exceptionally, by the King, to whom it agreed to make a substantial loan. Goya was commissioned to commemorate the occasion, unprecedented in the annals of Spanish business. He realized one of the most important paintings in the history of Spanish art, handling what was by nature a formal subject in a relaxed manner. The figures are placed in a palatial setting, space and light playing an essential role in the composition.

Goya is sometimes credited with rebellious social ideas not in keeping with his true political beliefs. In common with the majority of his friends and patrons – Jovellanos, Cabarrús, Yriarte, Moratín and many more – he inclined towards a constitutional monarchy, in the hope it would provide better government of Spain. He believed in a just and well-organized hierarchy, as reflected by his personal attachment to the post of Court Painter. At the same time he was convinced, particularly in the last fifteen years of his life, that there was no cure ('*no hubo remedio!*') for mankind's disastrous fate. Yet he himself had a tremendous zest for life and his optimistic nature was in perpetual struggle with the pessimism induced by his experiences. This often intense conflict generated surprising masterpieces: he would lightly approach the most serious of subjects – or those generally held to be serious, such as the famous *Assembly of the Company of the Philippines* (left) of 1815.

On the same occasion three influential members of the Company – Miguel de Lardizabal, Ignacio Omulryan and José Muñarriz – had individual portraits painted by Goya, in harmonizing monochromatic tones.

In contrast he marshalled the full effects of colour for his monumental *Portrait of the Duke of San Carlos*, the detestable minister and unwitting pawn of Talleyrand, who encouraged a love affair between his own wife and the Spanish duke.

The muddled policies of the King, an old-style despot who persecuted both the liberals and the *afrancesados* because they wanted a diminution of royal power, did little to restore order in a Spain cruelly ravaged by the war.

Goya was now approaching seventy and in 1815 painted a famous half-length self-portrait in which the years do not seem to have touched him. He had lost none

Goya closely followed the story of the saint's life in *The Last Communion of Saint Joseph of Calazanz* (right). Seriously ill, the saint had nonetheless got up from his sickbed for the last time to take communion on 10 August 1648. He was surrounded by his students and all the monks of the church of San Pantaleon in Rome, his faithful followers who loved him like a father. He died on 25 August, aged ninety-two.

Above left: 'The House of the Deaf Man'. Below: *The Tenth Duke of Osuna.*

of the combative spirit of his youth, going on to produce a pictorial saga on the national art of bullfighting, *Tauromachy*, engraved in 1816. The same year *The Caprices* went back on sale.

It was now the turn of the children of Goya's old patrons to be painted: *The Duchess of Abrantes*, wreathed in flowers, and her brother *The Tenth Duke of Osuna*, in relaxed pose. On 13 September 1817, probably intending to go away for a period, Goya gave a friend authorization to collect his salary as Court Painter. The same year he was commissioned to do a painting for the cathedral in Seville. He produced several preliminary drawings, having inspected the appointed site 'to assess distances, lighting and viewpoints': confirmation of his meticulous attention to perspective and composition. The eventual painting, installed in January 1818, was far removed from the expected devotional work: the two patron saints of Seville, Justa and Rufina, look like buxom *majas.*

Our first information for 1819 is that on 19 February, for 60,000 reals, Goya bought a country house, known, by an uncanny coincidence, as the 'House of the Deaf Man'. It lay beyond the Segovia bridge, towards the meadow of San Isidro.

The Black Paintings: magic and religion

In his country house, the 'House of the Deaf Man', on the walls of two large rooms, one above the other, Goya painted a series of vast compositions in oil and tempera onto the plaster itself: a veritable social manifesto and angry political protest in a period of great disturbances. The paintings are today in the Prado. Many historical studies have been devoted to the works and some are beginning to be better understood. *Asmodeus* or *Fantastic Vision* (above left) has always been read as a magic scene, but it can also be taken as a reference to the rock of Gibraltar, the shape of which resembles the rock in the picture; it was a refuge of the liberals between 1815 and 1833.

The composition *Fight with Cudgels* (below left) probably represents the biblical story of the brothers Cain and Abel: they came to blows in a field of wheat and sunk into it up to their knees – a possible allusion to the civil war in Spain.

The Black Paintings: murder and cannibalism

The biblical heroine Judith (opposite) seduced the enemy general Holofernes and cut off his head while he was sleeping, thus saving the Jewish people. Painting this heroic figure, Goya captures the perversity and cruelty of a woman who was capable of using her powers of seduction to disarm and destroy a man.

The Roman god Saturn wanted to reign alone. He dethroned his father and devoured his children to ensure he could never suffer his father's fate. Goya portrays him (left) devouring not his children but a fragile female body, probably a comment on the sexual appetite of the male.

The Black Paintings: witches and sorcerers

In *The Witches' Sabbath* (detail left) the figure of the goat is surrounded by a gathering of women, confirmation of Goya's belief that the female sex was more given to sorcery than the male. The scene symbolizes the primitive, almost animal superstition still very widespread in the Spain of the period.

❛Goya, nightmare full of things unknown,
The foetus that is cooked in the midst of the sabbaths,
Old women in the mirror and children all naked,
Adjusting their stockings to tempt the devils.❜

Charles Baudelaire
The Flowers of Evil
1857

After the death of his wife in 1812, Goya became involved with Leocadia Weiss, a young relative of his daughter-in-law Gumersinda Goicoechea, which caused trouble between Goya and his son Javier. In 1824 Leocadia went to Bordeaux to join Goya, taking her ten-year-old daughter Rosario with her. Goya and Leocadia were an argumentative couple, but the painter adored Rosario and taught her the rudiments of painting, finding she had a great natural aptitude. Leocadia is the model in this painting, *La Manola*.

In August 1819, when he painted *The Last Communion of Saint Joseph of Calazanz* for the Escuelas Pías in Madrid, the artist had no difficulty marrying realism and propriety. The subject naturally appealed to him, a ready vehicle for his profound religious feeling, and he rendered it with great poignance in the mystic tradition of the 17th century. He received 16,000 reals as payment and gave back 6800 'in tribute to his countryman Saint Joseph of Calazanz', also presenting the prior with a little canvas of *Christ in the Garden of Olives*, one of his great masterpieces. On 4 April 1820 Goya attended the last academic meeting of his career.

Probably encouraged by international freemasonry, the movement for constitutional reform re-emerged, to the growing alarm of the European monarchies. After the Congress of Verona (August 1822) France decided to send an expeditionary force in support of Ferdinand VII. In summer 1823 the constitutional armies were defeated outright and the King returned to power, determined to

This composition, known as *La Manola*, is one of the paintings originally to be found on the ground floor of the 'House of the Deaf Man'. Leocadia Weiss is seen leaning on a tomb provoking occasionally unsympathetic comments by historians on the funereal aspect of the lady. Recent radiographic studies have, however, shown that Goya painted Leocadia with her face uncovered leaning on a mantelpiece; and that the tomb and veil painted over the original are probably not by Goya's hand but added after his death.

take vengeance. On 17 September 1823 Goya suddenly made over the ownership of the 'House of the Deaf Man' to his grandson Mariano. Did he fear confiscation? Extensive scientific studies have revealed that Goya first decorated the walls of his house with vast landscapes which he later covered with the 'Black Paintings' today on view in the Prado Museum. It was probably between spring and summer 1823 that a fit of rebellion and despair seized him.

In the past three decades he had suffered the consequences of a European revolution, a foreign invasion and a civil war, and now felt driven to denounce on the walls of this house the enduring evil and incurable folly of man. Greatly concerned for his own safety he took refuge in winter 1823–4 with Father Duaso. In May 1824 he applied for permission to take the waters in France at Plombières, intending to settle in Bordeaux, a port trading with Spain, in which many of his friends, the *afrancesados*, were living.

For the first time Goya wants to leave his country for political reasons

He got to Bordeaux on 24 June, to be welcomed by his friend Moratín who described him as 'deaf, old, feeble, weak, not knowing a word of French, but so happy and eager to see the world'; Goya then headed straight for Paris, arriving on 30 June 1824. According to police reports he saw nobody, 'walked in public places and visited monuments'. We can only speculate about his reactions as a tourist in the French capital, where his own genius was unknown and unrecognized. He did a painting there of a bullfight and excellent portraits of his friend Joaquín Maria Ferrer and his wife. In September he returned to Bordeaux where he was joined by Leocadia Weiss and her daughter Rosario. As a 'young student', he applied himself to mastering the new technique of lithography, making the convincing *Portrait of the Printer Gaulon* and four famous plates entitled the *Bulls of Bordeaux*, in which he uses crayons, razor and scraper to achieve highly original effects of form, attitude and colour. The next year he was allowed an absence of six months, this time in Bagnères. Goya disrupted the life of the peaceable old Moratín, and 'enjoyed the city, the fields, the climate, the food, the independence and tranquillity he came across in Bordeaux'. 'If one let him,' said Moratín 'he would steal away on a mule with his beret, his cape, his stirrups, his boots and his knapsack.'

In May 1825 Goya became seriously ill again. Doctors diagnosed paralysis of the bladder and a large tumour of the perineum. He recovered, lost no time resuming work and produced some forty miniatures on ivory, at a stroke, 'correcting nothing'. He applied for an extension of his leave, this time for a year. In 1826, wearying of the French, he went to Madrid. He was eighty years old, and had to cover nine hundred

This painting, *The Milkmaid of Bordeaux*, is a hymn to youth by an artist who despite his age and infirmities has retained the feeling and imagination of his twenties. Rosario Weiss was fourteen when Goya painted this work, but there is no evidence that she was the model. Here he rediscovers his taste for brightness and blue sky. It is a fairy-tale image, combining grace and youth with the utmost naturalness.

Goya drew this *Self-portrait in a Cap* in 1824.

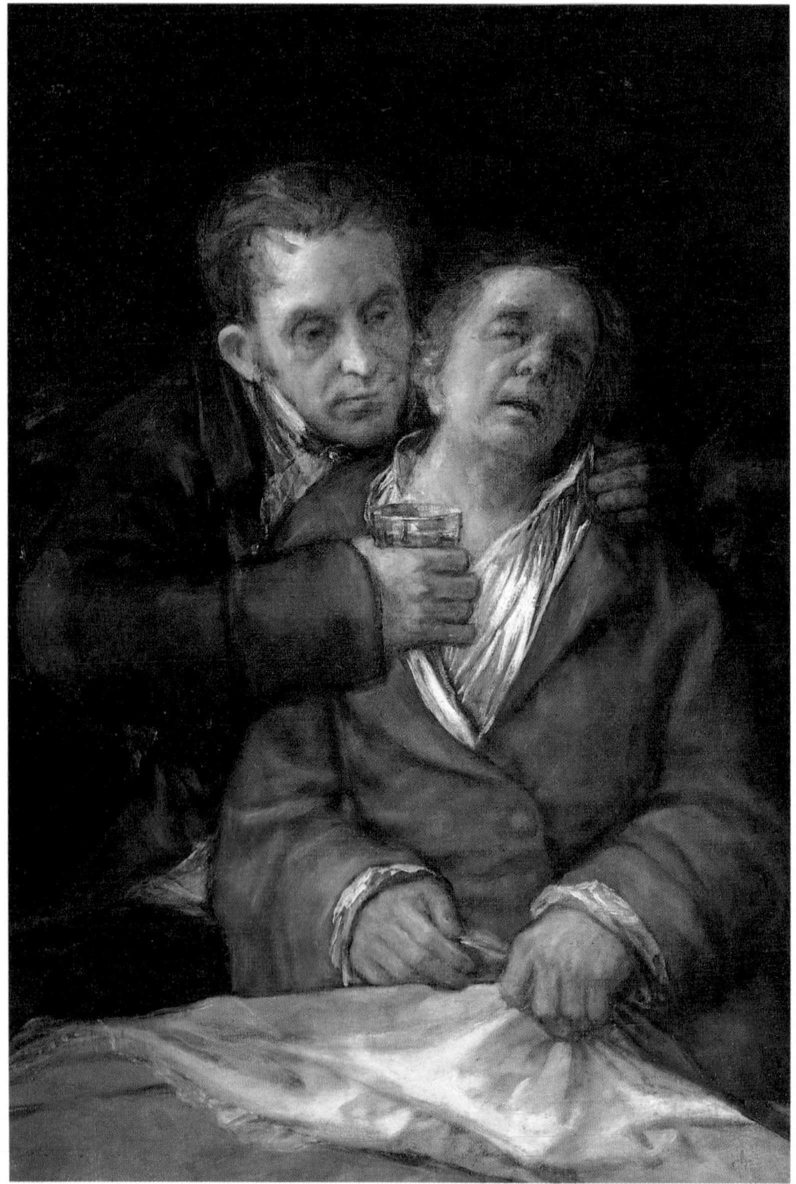

oya and his itics: Baudelaire

ya's work was first made own in France by Baron ylor, who founded the nous Musée Espagnol. t his genius was slow to n recognition: it was the ssical Velázquez who was arded as the great anish painter, not the tlandish Goya. In 1857, the paper Le Présent, *udelaire took up Goya's use and emphasized what as to become the basis of reputation: his interest the fantastic and horrific.*

❛ Linda Maestra. – A good teacher.❜

Goya is always a great artist, and often frightening. To the fundamentally gay and jocose spirit of Spanish satire, with its heyday in Cervantes' time, Goya has added something very much more modern, or rather a quality which has been particularly sought after in modern times, namely, a love of the indefinable, a feeling for violent contrasts, for what is terrifying in nature, and for human features which have acquired animal-like qualities as a result of their environment. It is curious to note that this spirit has manifested itself in the train of the great critical and satirical movement of the eighteenth century. Voltaire would have been grateful simply for the idea of all Goya's caricatures of monks... monks yawning, monks gorging, monks with square murderous heads preparing for matins, monks with cunning, hypocritical, sly and deceitful heads, like birds of prey in profile. It is strange that this monk-hater has dreamed so frequently of witches, sabbaths, devilry, children cooking on a spit, and I know not what else: all the orgies of the dream-world, all the exaggerations of hallucinatory images, and, in addition, all those slim, white Spanish girls, whom the inevitable old hags wash and make ready for their covens, or for the evening's prostitution – the sabbath of civilization! Light and darkness, reason and the irrational are played against each other in all these grotesque horrors. What an extraordinary sense of the comic!

I recall particularly two incredible plates. One shows a fantastic landscape, a mixture of rocks and cloud. Some lost and uninhabited corner of the sierras, perhaps, or a patch of primeval chaos? In the centre of this vile stage, a violent battle is in progress between two witches flying through the air. One sits astride the other; lambasting and overpowering her. These two monsters roll through a darkened

kilometres in uncomfortable conditions. He persuaded the Court to agree to his retirement at a pension of 50,000 reals, equal to his salary, and to allow him to return to France.

Back in Bordeaux he did a portrait of the banker Santiago Galos, who managed his affairs, and in May 1827 of the Spanish businessman Juan Bautista Muguiro, a relation of his daughter-in-law. The work is remarkable in its modernity and its almost palpable physicality. In summer 1827 he made his last trip to Madrid, where he painted the features of his beloved grandson Mariano, now an elegant young man, somewhat pugnacious and thoroughly undisciplined.

In Bordeaux again he realized his final masterpieces: a portrait of the former mayor of Madrid, *Pío de Molina,* and the exquisite *Milkmaid of Bordeaux*, a refreshing portrayal of the younger sister of one of the handsome *manolas* of old.

'I have no sight, no strength, no pen, no inkstand, all is wanting, only my willpower is left me'

In January 1828 Goya, with his customary energy and efficiency, prepared for the arrival of his son, who with his household was on the way to Paris. At the end of the winter he suffered another attack but recovered sufficiently to deal with a transfer of capital of 45,000 francs, a considerable sum at the period, into Mariano's name.

On 28 March he received his daughter-in-law and grandson. 'I am in bed, ill again', he wrote to Javier at the beginning of April, whose arrival he excitedly awaited, in spite of the fact that he was virtually at death's door. He had lightheartedly told him in 1824 that he might live like Titian until the age of ninety-nine. Fate dictated otherwise and Goya died on 16 April 1828 in the handsome apartment in the Fossés de l'Intendance at Bordeaux, under the sign of the Ram that had witnessed his birth eighty-two years earlier.

This self-portrait with his doctor, Arrieta (left), is dedicated to the latter 'in gratitude for his success and the great care he has taken saving my life during the violent and dangerous illness I suffered in late 1819, at the age of seventy-three'.

On the back of this portrait of his twenty-one year-old grandson Mariano, Goya inscribed the fact that he was eighty-one, as if amazed to be still at work.

❛The colours of [Goya's] apparitions have no more *raison d'être* than his paintings... he foreshadows all modern art, because modern art begins with this freedom.❜

André Malraux
Saturn, 1950

DOCUMENTS

Goya and his critics.
Goya's engravings.
The private Goya.

'Están calientes. – They are hot.'

Charles Baudelaire.

atmosphere. All the ugliness, all the moral degradation, all the vices which the mind can imagine are written on their two faces which seem half beast, half human, as is common in Goya – though the technique he uses to achieve the effect is inexplicable.

The other plate shows an unfortunate being – a solitary, desperate human atom, trying his hardest to escape from his tomb. Maleficent devils, hundreds of loathsome Lilliputian gnomes unite their efforts to keep down the lid of the half-open grave. These vigilant watchmen of death join forces against the recalcitrant soul which wears itself out in the impossible struggle. This nightmare scene is enacted against the full horror of an indescribable and featureless background.

At the end of his life, Goya's eyesight had grown so feeble that they say his pencils had to be sharpened for him. Nevertheless, even at that stage he produced some large lithographs of considerable importance, including bull-fights full of massing figures. These wonderful plates – miniature versions of huge canvases – give new evidence of the force of the law which rules the destinies of great artists, and which decrees that their life runs in some inverse proportion to their intelligence. They gain on the one hand what they lose on the other, and grow younger all the time, gaining in strength, vigour and daring, until they reach the very edge of the tomb itself.

In the foreground of one of these lithographs, in which an admirable sense of tumult and confusion reigns, a maddened bull – one of those vengeful creatures which attack the dead with unprecedented violence – has ripped the seat of the trousers of one of the combatants, who, wounded but not killed, drags himself heavily along on his knees. The formidable beast, which has already torn the unfortunate man's shirts to shreds with its horns, and exposed his naked posterior, now lowers his head again in a menacing way. And yet the crowd is hardly moved at all by this scene of blatant carnage.

The chief merit of Goya lies in his ability to create credible monstrosities. His monsters are viable, harmoniously proportioned. No one has dared to go further than he in the direction of grotesque reality. All these contortions, bestial faces, and diabolical grimaces, are profoundly human. Even from the technical point of view of natural history, it would be hard to fault them, every inch of them is so well-knit and so carefully integrated into the whole. In a word, it is difficult to say precisely at what point reality and fantasy are knitted together and joined. The border-line between the two is so skilfully crossed that the subtlest analysis cannot trace it; the art behind it is so natural, yet so transcendental also.

Charles Baudelaire
Le Présent, 1857

'Y aún no se van! – And still they don't go!'

Goya and his critics: Mérimée

Goya drew criticism on every count: for his drawing (totally without technical skill), his colouring (totally unlifelike) and, more generally, his subjects – the fantastic was held in disregard for much of the 19th century, notwithstanding romantic taste for morbidity and excess. Thus Prosper Mérimée, a writer well-acquainted with Spain, expressed his utter antipathy to Goya's phantasmagoria.

I cannot forgive you for admiring Goya. I had no idea that he had ever been in love with the Duchess of Alba, whom he painted in a yellow shift and transparent dress. But I find nothing in the least pleasing about his paintings or his etchings. It is true that his plates after Velázquez are useful reminders of the original paintings if one knows these already. But how can you possibly consider *The Disasters of War* aesthetically satisfying? He couldn't even draw bulls properly, despite his interest in bull-fighting as an *aficionado*. The *Caprichos* he etched when he was more than half insane have some fairly good imaginative and humorous touches. And it is not so much the subjects as the technique of his paintings that disgusts me. If one wants to break academic rules and take a plunge into the realities of ordinary life, one must at least start by copying nature. Goya, on the other hand, would put colours on to his palette without rhyme or reason, and when he found a range of tones to his liking, that was the end of the painting. It would have been better if he had left the patches of colour as they were, and not tried to make figures out of them. Did you go to *Las Delicias*? It's one of the Duke of Osuna's country houses, inherited from his aunt the Duchess of Benavente. Goya painted a series of life-size scenes of witchcraft in it, after the manner of the *Caprichos*. There is a witch changing into a goat that made an impression on me. But to conclude, if one wants to be a realist, in my view one should either follow Velázquez, or leave the whole thing alone.

Prosper Mérimée
Letter to Duchess Colonna
16 May 1869

'Aguarda que te unten. – Wait till you've been anointed.'

Goya and his critics: Malraux

In 1950 André Malraux wrote the essay Saturn *on the subject of Goya, with the express aim of 'coming to grips with one of the most desperate of the spiritual quests of the West'. The last chapter deals with the artist's old age, exiled in France, deaf, ill, virtually blind, but ever dedicated to his art, producing paintings, engravings, lithographs...*

The providential discovery of lithography (his weakened eyes no longer allowed him to etch) transformed his drawing. It had always been open to experiment but also it was too much the preparation for and the result of his engraving not to be affected by the radical changes in the latter. His patches of colour become more blurred, his accents less sharp. As much as ever he shuns Italian over-refinement, now neo-classical, but his style is hesitant before the stone, as was that of all the early lithographers.

Between his idea (or his model) and his pencil drawing there seems to be interposed a sepia from an earlier period, a sepia of which the drawing would be a faltering copy. His etchings had been simply engravings – his compositions and portraits are only paintings; but his drawings are based on a line which is unsteady and slightly crushed, and often of a lightness in colour similar to that of the engravings in which he had employed the technique of Tiepolo. He seems to be going back to his youth; as indeed he was, until the day when he discovered that the basis of lithography is not only black but white as well.

He had made that discovery once before in etching. At Bordeaux, where he could not take his painted monsters, he drew them again, but in his faltering drawing they also grew old... Yet once again, as at San Fernando, as with the darkness of the *Caprichos*, he hit upon it. By first spreading all over the stone a grey from which he would tear the patches of white with a scraper, he recaptured the black, the basis, the line so passionately authoritative – the accent of his colour. He stood the stone like a canvas on his easel. He gave up sharpening his pencils but used them like brushes. He strove for that effect of a composed unity which demands to be seen at a distance, the

‘Disparate ridículo. – Ridiculous folly.’

effect he had sought in his pictures but which no one for a long time to come would demand from lithography. And he ended by using the magnifying glass, not because of care for detail, which he avoided – but because his eyes were going...

As to the faltering hand of the drawings executed with a sharpened pencil, that becomes the old majestic scrawl. Not to produce monsters now, but to satisfy the other abiding passion of his life, the one he had known before the phantoms and against which they had not prevailed; even beneath the cry of anguish he had heard the muffled gong of blood. Here once again is the echo of the stilled clamour of war, the echo of the age-old voice of the Spain he had left behind – the bull.

He had previously devoted forty plates to it and many pictures. The *Tauromachia* was a wonderful collection. In spite of an apparent repetition where genius seemed to be wearing thin, each one of the compositions, with the exception of a few documentary plates (and even in them his hall-mark is not absent), had found again the grand manner. In every corrida there is the mixture of a spectacle from the circus (with its element of danger, but acrobats also are killed sometimes) and a communion in blood. Goya went from spectacle to communion, from the *aficionado*'s pleasure to the celebration of a sacrifice. His other-worldly black was as much a part of his dealings with death as it had been of his witchcraft. And the bull, whatever the subject of the engravings may have been, was always the bull. Harassed by dogs, picadors, and banderilleros, it never lost that pent-up immobility that Goya gave it so forcibly as it confronted the lances, the immobility that was to hurl itself into slaughter – on the scarcely lowered horns eviscerated horses or dead men would writhe in the succeeding plates. In the art of *Francisco de los Torros* what part had not been played by the combination of death, sport, and the dark side of the world! Certainly the corrida, its costumes, and its sacrifice were in his eyes a blood-stained carnival. From so many forgotten accidents and exploits there remained, when the album was closed, the silhouette, heroic in its animal fashion, that so often was to be seen against the sky above the ridges of Aragon, just as in times past the Minotaur had arisen before the slopes of the headlands of Crete.

Yet even the bulls now lose the muscular bronze sheen that etching gave them. Goya searched gropingly for the sparkle that his painting would find. For he still went on painting in that poignant light in which the approach of death brings together Titian, Hals, Rembrandt, and Michelangelo, old men weary of life but not of painting, turned away at last from mankind and painting only for themselves. Painters know old age but their painting does not... He worked at his last portraits, at the *Nun*, and the *Monk*. His haunted loneliness, a loneliness haunted now by the eternal as well, had joined the deafness he shared with Beethoven. But his drawings were exhausted. He would have to change their style and find, in gouache no doubt, the equivalent of the whiteness of the scraped stone. He passed through Paris, saw – and disregarded – the *Massacres of Scio*. He drew the man-skeleton, the charmer of lizards and snakes, and the idiot; then, again, some flying dogs and a few laggard demons. Spain herself was remote from him, the Spain of which he knew that if he had not painted her she would not be the same in the imagination of mankind... Yet she alone still knew him. A few artists alone realized that he was something besides a king of the picturesque. The reason is that only to Spaniards was the Spanish element in his work sometimes modern and sometimes nationalist but never exotic. In English and French eyes his mantillas, his monks and his tortures belonged to the theatre, almost to the imaginary. To Paris, a garrotted man was something

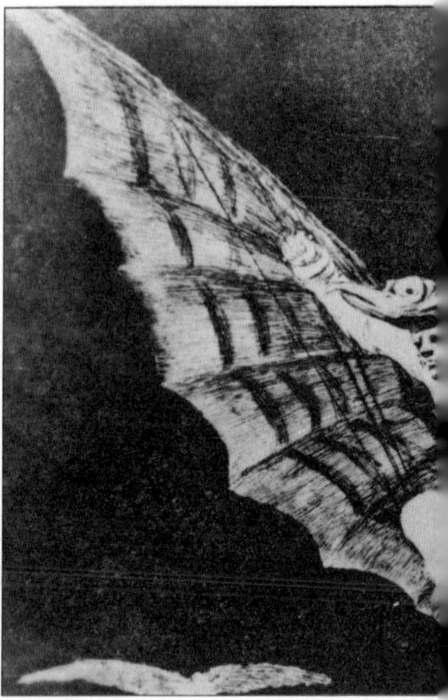

unreal – a man guillotined would not have been. (He drew the guillotine, as it happens, but for himself alone, and without rediscovering his genius.) To London, the figure in the *Monk's Visit* was first and foremost a monk; to Madrid it was the age-old apparition come from the world of the dead to demand justice, the apparition whose noiseless immobility puts to silence all the stir of human life and even the far-off rumble of the sea. He thought of new *Caprichos*; he had 'some better ideas than before'. His flattened manner now shatters the formalism of the *Agony in the Garden*, the shell-like coverings of the priests in the *Last Communion of St. Joseph of Calasanz* and in the *Mass for New-born Children*. A succession of paintings from which no picture could come, a style which aims not at light but at a powdering of colours to which

'Modo de volar. – A way of flying.'

Monticelli would later try to find the answer like a feeble echo of sadness, this is what emerges from his faltering drawings. The bulls with crows for riders that passed across the sky, the bulls that fell from it in rain in one of the later *Disparates*, reappear, scarcely discernible, in the epic hallucination of the last *Corrida*. He scarcely saw any more the world he heard no more; he began to be unable to see even his sketches... The stout *Water Carrier* becomes the *Milkmaid of Bordeaux* – we see the tremulous hand of the later Titians.

Soon painters would forget at the cost of what anguish this man had ranged his solitary and hopeless art against the entire civilization into which he had been born. From those still dazzling embers they would retain only the advent of the individual, the metamorphosis of the world in pictures. And yet...

'In such a night as this,...' In such a night the aged exile, whose deafness sent him to the fairs and roundabouts so as to avoid the gossip parties that brought his companions together at the house of the Valencian chocolate maker, still tried to make audible once again that voice that was the most eager for the absolute and the most remote from it that art has ever known. Perhaps it was on such a night that as he drew, half blind, the *Sleeping Giant*, he remembered that out of the anguish that never ends, beyond the dark cries of demons possessed in their turn, he had plucked the other *Giant* whose anxious face dreams amid the stars...

And now modern painting begins.

André Malraux
Saturn, 1957
Translation by C.W. Chilton

'El caballo raptor. – Equine abductor.'

'Disparate puntual. – Exact folly.'

'Bobalicon. – Buffoon.'

'Disparate matrimonial. – Matrimonial folly.'

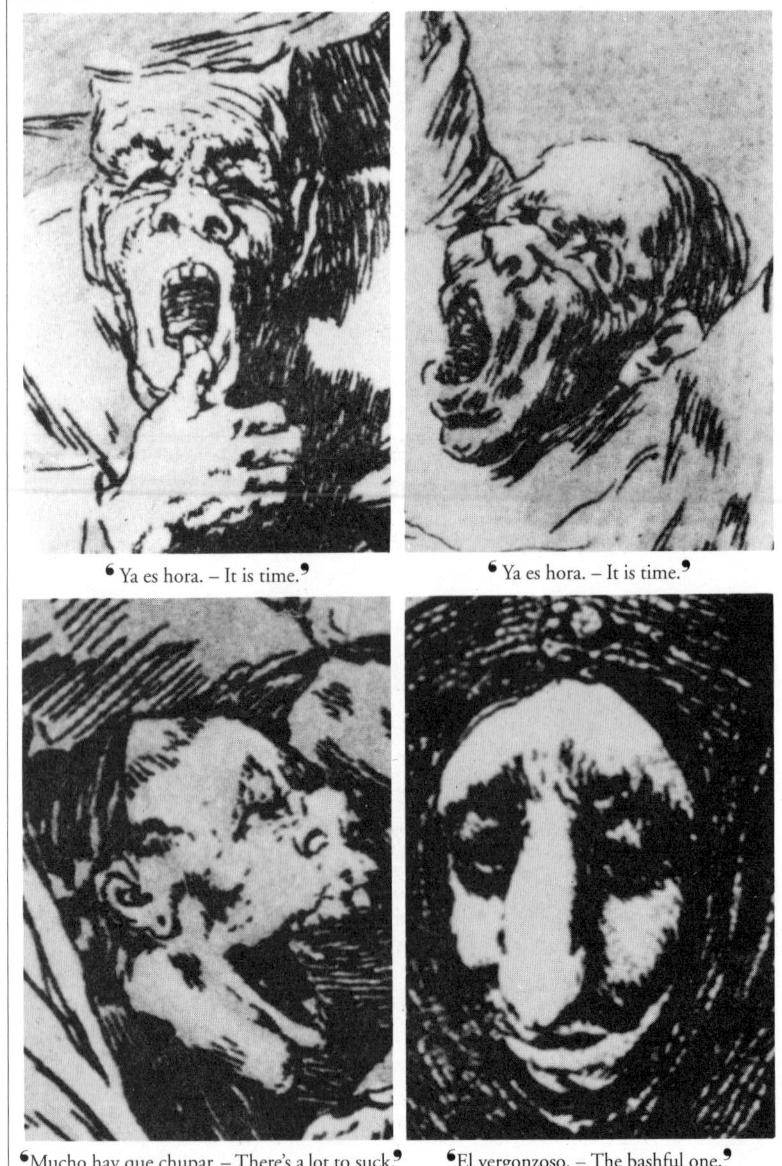

‘Ya es hora. – It is time.’

‘Ya es hora. – It is time.’

‘Mucho hay que chupar. – There's a lot to suck.’

‘El vergonzoso. – The bashful one.’

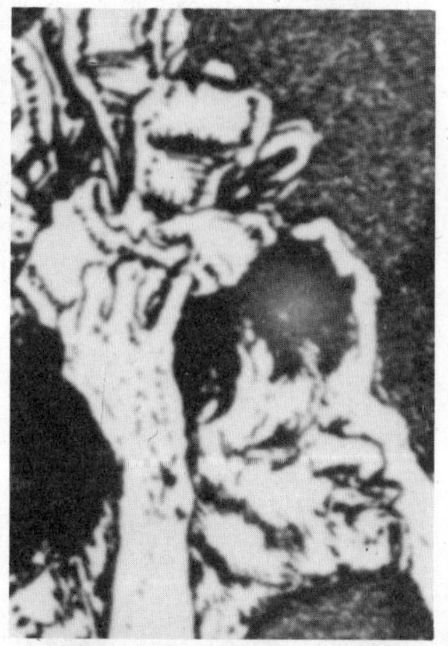

'Hasta la muerte. – Until death.'

'Duendecitos. – Hobgoblins.'

'Se repulen. – They spruce themselves up.'

'Hilan delgado. – They spin finely.'

Goya and *The Family of Charles IV*

Ever since Théophile Gautier described the figures in Goya's group portrait as 'the corner baker and his wife after they won the lottery', scholars, amateurs, and casual visitors to the Prado have asked themselves how it was possible for Goya's royal patrons to accept so degrading a portrait.... Goya's portrait ... remains unique in its drastic description of human bankruptcy.

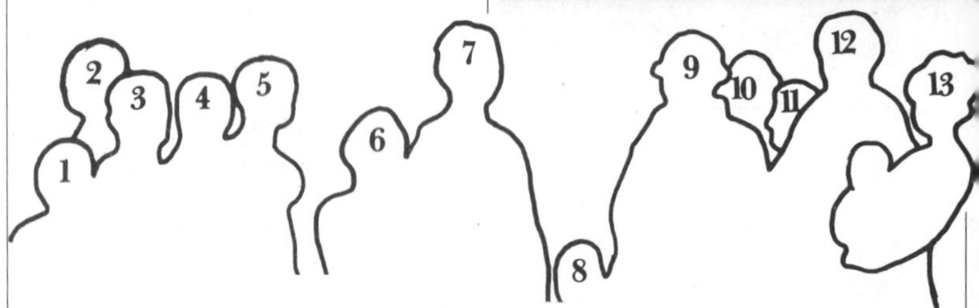

The Family of Charles IV. 1: Infante Carlos María Isidro. 2: Goya, the artist. 3: Infante Fernando. 4: Infanta María Josefa. 5: unknown. 6: Infanta María Isabel. 7: Queen María Luisa. 8: Infante Francisco de Paula. 9: King Charles IV. 10: Infante Antonio Pascual. 11: unknown. 12: Prince of Parma. 13: Princess of Parma and her child.

Portraits – especially ceremonial portraits – are, at least to some degree, monuments. The artist, for reasons he makes obvious, recommends his sitter to us as worthy of our regard and as something more than the mere sum of physiogenic feature. Goya was the first artist to rob the portrait of its magic, transcendental properties. From his day, portraiture was the genre most deeply affected by the spiritual upheavals of the 19th century. It never recovered its former power and popularity.

How a portrait of such fiercely intransigent realism was acceptable to its sitters is only one of a number of puzzles that surround this crucial work. Another arises from the peculiar location of the artist, behind, instead of in front of, his sitters. Most important of all, one must consider the significance of Goya's seemingly clumsy use of a compositional prototype: Velázquez's *Las Meninas.* A single glance at the general construction of the two paintings is enough to prove this universally accepted fact. In both pictures the painter himself stands behind a slightly inclined canvas at stage left; in both, the prospect is closed off by two large canvases hung on the rear wall; in both, the major figures are disposed in a very loose arrangement centring on a female figure brilliantly costumed (the infanta in the Velázquez, Maria Luisa in the Goya), who, with her head slightly cocked, stares straight out of the picture....

Without going too deeply into the problems *Las Meninas* poses to current scholarship, it is safe to say that the thematic and compositional core of the picture is bound up with the presence of the mirror behind the group in the foreground, in which the parents of the infanta are reflected. The insistent stares of Velázquez, the infanta, and the chamberlain in the background give the entire painting an element of suspense which is resolved by the putative presence of the king and queen, who stand (according to the reflection) somewhere outside the picture. Were it not for the mirror, which tells us what the cynosure of the major figures is, *Las Meninas* would be inexplicable.

In the Goya, too, the attentive glances of most of the portrait sitters are just as strongly focused on an object outside the picture. In fact, Maria Josefa, the king's grotesque old sister, pokes her head forward in purposeful, birdlike curiosity. But we look in vain for the one object that might yield a clue as to what all these people are looking at. After all the trouble to which Goya has gone to base his composition on *Las Meninas*, he withholds the one element that makes *Las Meninas* take on meaning: he withholds the mirror and the telltale reflection.

Or does he? Perhaps the very absence of the key element in *The Family of Charles IV* is deliberately meant to irritate us into finding the mirror that Goya has so sardonically hidden. Perhaps his superficially clumsy reference to *Las Meninas* was purposeful after all. We must at least hunt for the mirror in the hope that if it is found, it will do for the Goya what it did for the Velázquez: deliver the answer to one of the most disturbing group portraits ever painted....

New possibilities begin to appear in *The Family of Charles IV* if one transfers the idea of the mirror...to the royal group portrait. For one thing, the otherwise inexplicable position of Goya behind his sitters begins to make good sense if he is presumed to be portraying them from their reflection in a mirror, instead of from a direct confrontation, which would be impossible given his position *behind* his subjects. The previously vexing problem of Goya's plagiarization of Velázquez is also solved. The mirror is still there, but it is no longer within the picture. It *is* the picture.

The original question concerning the acceptability of such an unflattering group portrait is now no longer quite so enigmatic. The reason lies in the intricate situation he has set up, which is derived from the common procedure used in self-portraits. Goya has not presented his sitters as *he* saw them. He has presented them as they saw themselves. He records the unimpeachable evidence provided by the mirror image. The hard fact of this reflection is witnessed by the sitters themselves....

There is a suspicious awkwardness about each figure in Goya's painting that tells us immediately that the king doesn't know how a king is supposed to bear himself. He doesn't know how to be himself because he doesn't know who he is. Only the children in the portrait can look themselves in the face without assuming forced and false attitudes.

Fred Licht
Goya: The Origins of the Modern Temper in Art, 1980

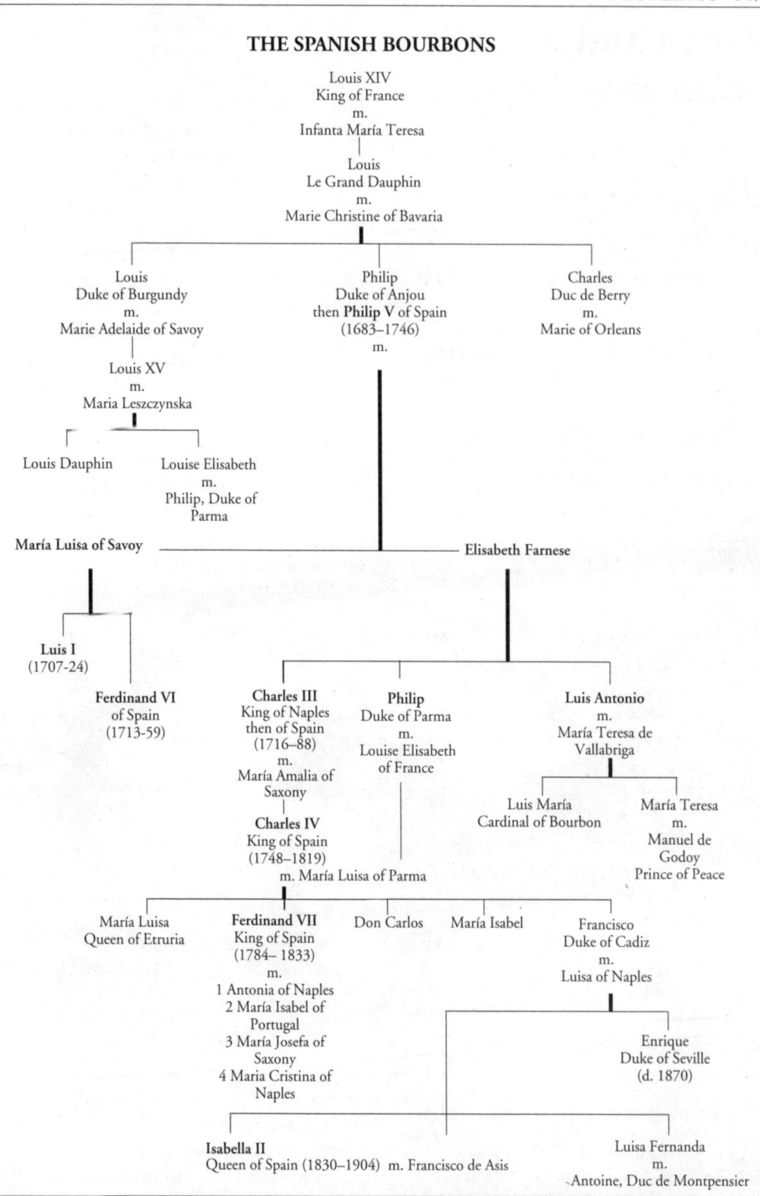
THE SPANISH BOURBONS
Louis XIV
King of France
m.
Infanta María Teresa
Louis
Le Grand Dauphin
m.
Marie Christine of Bavaria
Louis
Duke of Burgundy
m.
Marie Adelaide of Savoy
Philip
Duke of Anjou
then Philip V of Spain
(1683–1746)
m.
Charles
Duc de Berry
m.
Marie of Orleans
Louis XV
m.
Maria Leszczynska
Louis Dauphin
Louise Elisabeth
m.
Philip, Duke of Parma
María Luisa of Savoy
Elisabeth Farnese
Luis I
(1707-24)
Ferdinand VI
of Spain
(1713-59)
Charles III
King of Naples
then of Spain
(1716–88)
m.
María Amalia of Saxony
Philip
Duke of Parma
m.
Louise Elisabeth
of France
Luis Antonio
m.
María Teresa de Vallabriga
Luis María
Cardinal of Bourbon
María Teresa
m.
Manuel de Godoy
Prince of Peace
Charles IV
King of Spain
(1748–1819)
m. María Luisa of Parma
María Luisa
Queen of Etruria
Ferdinand VII
King of Spain
(1784– 1833)
m.
1 Antonia of Naples
2 María Isabel of Portugal
3 María Josefa of Saxony
4 Maria Cristina of Naples
Don Carlos
María Isabel
Francisco
Duke of Cadiz
m.
Luisa of Naples
Enrique
Duke of Seville
(d. 1870)
Isabella II
Queen of Spain (1830–1904) m. Francisco de Asis
Luisa Fernanda
m.
Antoine, Duc de Montpensier

Goya and *Tauromachy*

The Spanish War of Independence left its mark on the imagination of the French, who saw Spain as a nation in the grip of savagery, superstition and witchcraft, indulging its bloodthirst in the bullfight – a spectacle illustrated by Goya and described by Prosper Mérimée.

The bull, purposely irritated in the pen beforehand, rushes out furiously. Usually he reaches the middle of the place at a bound and there stops short, astonished by the noise he hears and the scene round about him. He wears on his neck a knot of ribbons hooked into the skin. The colour of these ribbons indicates what herd (*vacada*) he comes from; but an experienced amateur, without looking at them, can tell to which province and breed he belongs.

The *chulos* approach, wave their brilliant capes, and try to draw the bull toward one of the picadors. If the beast is game, it attacks him unhesitatingly. The picador, with the lance under his arm, gathers his horse well under him; takes his place exactly in front of the bull; seizes the moment at which the head is lowered for the charge to fix the lance in the neck, and not elsewhere; bears down with the full weight of his body and at the same time wheels his horse to the left, so as to leave the bull on the right. If all these movements are well executed, if the picador is vigorous and his horse

‘Desjarette de la canalla con lanzas, medias lunas, banderillas, y otras armas. – The rabble hamstring the bull with lances, sickles, *banderillas* and other arms.’

'Banderillas de fuego. – *Banderillas* with firecrackers.'

responsive, the bull, carried by his own impetus, goes by without touching him. Then the duty of the *chulos* is to distract the bull until the picador has had time to get out of the way, but often the animal knows only too well which is his real aggressor; brusquely he swings about, makes for the horse at a rush, and runs his horns into the belly, overthrowing both horse and rider. The latter is immediately rescued by the *chulos*. Some pick him up, others wave their capes before the bull's eyes, draw him toward themselves, and, leaping over the barrier with surprising agility, make their escape. The Spanish bull is as fast as a horse; and, if the *chulo* is far away from the fence, he barely reaches it. Therefore, the horseman, whose life must depend on the *chulos'* agility, does not often venture into the middle of the ring; when he does, it passes for an extraordinary feat of daring.

Once again on his feet, the picador, if he can get his horse up, remounts. Though the poor beast may be losing streams of blood, though its entrails drag on the ground and twine about its legs, it must face the bull as long as it can stand. When it is down to stay, the picador leaves the ring and returns immediately on a fresh mount.

I have said that the lances can only make a flesh-wound and serve only to infuriate the bull. Nevertheless, the impact of the horse and the rider, the bull's own efforts, above all the shock of pulling up short on his hocks, tire him rather promptly. Often, also, the pain of the lance-wounds disheartens him. At last, he no longer dares attack the horses, or, to use the technical term, he refuses to 'enter'. By that time, if he is vigorous, he has already killed four or five horses. The picadors rest; the signal is given to plant the *banderillas*.

These are sticks about two and a half feet long wrapped in strips of paper, with a sharp point which is barbed in order to stay in the wound. The *chulos* hold one of these darts in each hand. The most effective way to use them is to come up softly behind the bull and to strike the *banderillas* together suddenly. The startled bull turns about at once and charges. Just

Origen de los arpones o banderillas. – Origin of the harpoons or *banderillas.*

as, with lowered head, he reaches the *chulo*, the latter plants both *banderillas* at once on either side of his neck. This can be done only by remaining for an instant right in front of him and almost between his horns; then, slipping aside, letting him go by and flying for safety. A distraction, a movement of hesitation or of fright, and the man would be lost.... If by mischance he falls while planting the *banderillas*, he must not try to rise, but lie where he is, motionless. The bull rarely gores a man on the ground, not at all out of generosity, but because he closes his eyes as he charges, and goes over him without seeing him. Sometimes, however, he stops, sniffs him to make sure he is dead, then, drawing back several steps, lowers his head to toss him. But at this moment the *banderillo*'s comrades gather about, and distract the beast until he abandons the supposed corpse.

When the bull is cowardly and will not take four thrusts of the lance, the accepted number, the spectators, sovereign judges, condemn him by acclamation to a sort of torture – at the same time a punishment and a means of reviving his fury. From all sides goes up a cry of '*Fuego! Fuego!*' Then, instead of their ordinary arms, the *chulos* are given *banderillas* with fire-crackers along the shaft and a piece of light amadou at the top. As soon as it enters the skin, the amadou lights the fuse: the explosives go off toward the bull, burning him to the quick, and, greatly to the satisfaction of the public, he leaps and plunges. It is, in fact, an admirable sight: this enormous animal, foaming with rage, shaking the flaming sticks, and tossing amid fire and smoke. In spite of milords the poets, I must say that of all the animals I have observed, none has less expression in its eyes than the bull. I should say, *changes* its expression less; for the bull's is almost always that of brutal and savage stupidity. Rarely does he express his pain by groaning: wounds enrage or frighten him, but never, if it may be said, does he seem to reflect upon his fate; he never weeps like the stag. Therefore, he inspires pity only when his

‘El animoso moro Gazul es el primero que lanceó toro en regla. – The spirited Moor Gazul is the first to spear bulls according to rules.’

‘Ligereza y atrevimiento de Juanito Apiñani en la de Madrid. – The agility and audacity of Juanito Apiñani in [the ring at] Madrid.’

'Pedro Romero matando a toro parado. – Pedro Romero killing the halted bull.'

courage is worthy of remark.

Three or four pairs of *banderillas* having been placed in the bull's neck, the time has come to make an end of him. There is a roll of drums. Immediately, the matador, one of the *chulos*, steps forth from among his comrades. Richly clad with gold and silk, he holds a long sword and a scarlet cloak, fastened to a stick so that it may be handled conveniently. This is called the *muleta*. He pauses under the President's box, and with a low bow asks permission to kill the bull. Usually this formality takes places only once for the whole performance. Of course the President nods his consent. The matador cries, '*Viva*', pirouettes, throws his hat on the ground, and advances to meet the bull.

Like duelling, these combats are governed by rules, to infringe which is as infamous as to kill one's adversary treacherously. For example, the matador may strike the bull only where the neck and the back join; the Spaniards call this place the 'cross'. The blow must be dealt from above, as one would say, 'in second'; never from below. A thousand times better lose one's life, than to thrust from below, from the side, or from behind. The matador's sword is long, strong, and double-edged; the hilt, very short, ends in a ball which is pressed against the palm of the hand. The use of this weapon calls for long experience and peculiar skill.

To kill a bull well, one must understand its character thoroughly. Upon this knowledge depends not only a matador's glory, but his life. As one may imagine, there are as many different natures among bulls as among men; however, they are divided into two distinct groups, the 'clear' and the 'obscure' – this is the language of the arena. The 'clear' attack openly; the 'obscure', on the other hand, are cunning, and try to get their man treacherously. The latter are extremely dangerous.

Before attempting the sword-thrust, the matador displays the *muleta*, excites the bull, and attentively observes whether he throws himself upon it, or whether he comes up quietly, in order to gain ground, and to charge only when the adversary

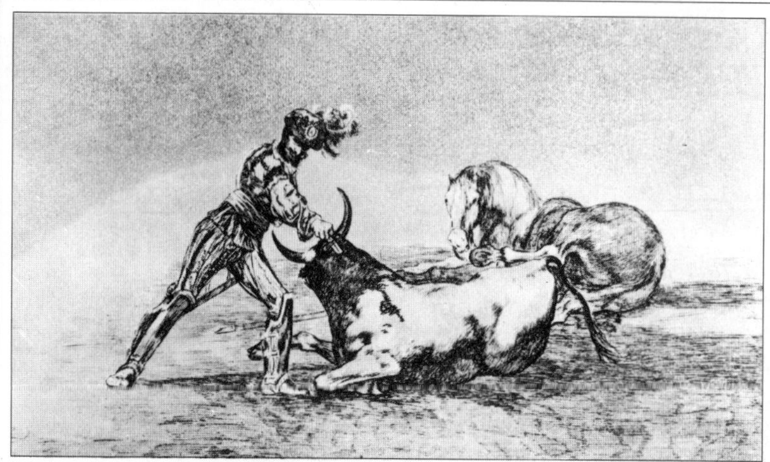

'Un caballero español mata un toro después de haber perdido el caballo. – A Spanish knight kills the bull after having lost his horse.'

seems too near to avoid the impact. Often the bull is seen to shake his head menacingly, to paw the ground without wanting to come forward, or even to draw back slowly, in an attempt to draw the man to the middle of the ring where he cannot escape. Others, instead of attacking in a straight line, sidle up, feigning exhaustion; but having measured their distance, lunge straight at the man.

For one who understands the art of bull-fighting, this is an interesting sight: the approaches of the matador and the bull who, like two skilful generals, seem to divine each other's plans and to vary their technique, moment by moment. For an experienced matador, a movement of the head, a sidelong look, a lowered ear, are so many plain indications of his enemy's projects. Finally, the impatient bull throws himself upon the red flag behind which the matador hides. His force is sufficient to batter down a wall with his horns; but the man slips aside with a light movement; disappears as if by magic; and defying the bull's fury, leaves only a light cloth uplifted over his head. The impetus of the animal carries him far beyond his opponent; then he stops, pulling up short on stiffened legs; and these abrupt and violent reflexes tire him so greatly that if the procedure were continued, it would be enough to kill him.... After a number of passes, the matador understands his antagonist thoroughly, and prepares to give the final thrust. He stands firmly, immobile, at the proper distance. The sword is held in the right hand, the right elbow at the height of the head; the left arm holds the *muleta* out in front where, almost on the ground, it induces the bull to lower his head. This is the moment that the matador gives the mortal thrust with all the force of his arm; and if the thrust is well-directed the man has nothing more to fear: the bull stops short; the blood scarcely flows; he lifts his head; his legs tremble, and he collapses in a great mass. Immediately the arena rings with deafening '*Vivas!*'.

Prosper Mérimée
Letters from Spain, 1931

Goya and *The Disasters of War*

The series of etchings which Goya called The Disasters of War *grew directly from a historical event, the guerilla war, waged by the Spanish people against the French between 1808 and 1814. But they are in another sense the least historical of Goya's works. They align rather with the raw suffering of televison or news photographs from Vietnam, Northern Ireland or Bosnia.*

'No se puede mirar. – One can't look.'

The executioners we do not see. Their rifles thrust in from the right, sharp with bayonets, inhuman and implacable. The eye follows their thrust, from a twilit grey into a blackness. Who are these huddled people? They are ordinary, common; their probably unremarkable lives are ending now in brutal, wanton, faceless killing. They die without heroism or dignity and yet there is something inexpressible about the manner of their dying which makes it an obscenity.

One man kneels in prayer, face turned from the rifles. Another, nearer to us, looks at them in futile entreaty. Between the men, light cuts through to a cowled woman huddling protectively over a child, to a face buried in hands, to a woman stretched in despair on black ground; the light spears home on the natural target on the pivoting eye, a woman of the people, distraught, kneeling, arms thrown out, face lifting to the black and unresponsive sky. 'One can't look' says the caption. But one must.

It could be anywhere; it could be My Lai. The caption, however, is in Spanish; the engraver is Francisco Goya. So we know that the rifles are French and that this is the War of Spanish Independence of 1808–14: the first guerilla war, the first 'people's war' of modern history, which was also the first of Spain's modern civil wars.
The martyred people are the Spanish *pueblo*....

Here are the French again, the humped figures of soldier-murderers, like some kind of collective animal, thrusting their bayonets – and confronting them, two of the *pueblo* jabbing with makeshift spear and dagger. They have faces, they are human, they are the *pueblo* in arms in defence

‘Con razon ó sin ella. – With or without reason.’

‘Nada. Ello dirá. – Nothing. That’s what it says.’

'Ya no hay tiempo! – There is no time now!'

'Que hay que hacer mas? – What more can one do?'

'Fuerte cosa es! – It's a hard thing!'

of their homes, their women, their religion, their country. There is something of the heroic about them. But they are totally unidealized. It is plain killing.

This is one of the first of the great and terrible series of engravings which Goya made during and after the war of 1808–14 and which have passed into common parlance as *The Disasters of War*. They stand almost without equal as a record of the pitiless inhumanity and more, the purposelessness of war, when all causes and creeds in the end sink into a morass of murder. Their technical skill is superb, the massing of shapes, the textures, the play of light and shade. Even the horrors are coldly beautiful.

One strength lies in their apparent evocation of direct experience. All extraneous details are pared away; there are no subplots. Groups of people are pinpointed in light, centre, within the scene. We stand within a few yards of them, as they shovel corpses into a pit, strip the dead, patch up the wounded, carry off the corpses of famine. We stand even closer as men are hanged; we can see their faces screw up, their tongues start from their heads. Men are spitted on tree trunks, dismembered, strangled; women are raped again and again, within touching distance. We look over a soldier's shoulder as he carves a sword into a man's groin....

In the end, we can't tell one side from the other, they grow into frightful beasts and monsters. The ejection of the French is followed by the restoration of the Spanish monarchy which immediately drives Spain back into black and remorseless reaction. It is the ultimate deception. A corpse, half-buried, half-skeleton, scrawls a message from the grave – *Nada*. 'Nothing. That's what it says'.

Gwyn A. Williams
Goya and the Impossible Revolution, 1976

Goya and *The Third of May, 1808*

The Third of May, 1808 (pp. 8–9) is such a powerful and realistic painting that it is natural to see it as the record of an eyewitness. It is probably not that, though it is certain that Goya saw many of the horrors that he later depicted in The Disasters of War. *Politically, however, he had no great hopes for the Spanish people even if the French were defeated.*

In 1808, Goya lived in the Calle Valverde, no. 15. The street, though not the house, survives behind the telephone building. Thus he could not have been, as is sometimes said, a witness from his actual windows of the events of 2 May; nor could he have seen the shootings of 3 May from any house of his own (he did not buy the *Quinta del Sordo*, 'the country house of the deaf man' until 1819). But where exactly he was on 2 May and 3 May is not known.

The first French soldier (a mameluke) to be killed in the Puerta del Sol was apparently shot by a bullet coming from a window of the house of a certain Gabriel Bález, who was a relation by marriage of Goya's daughter-in-law. Goya's son was also apparently living very close to the Puerta del Sol. No one can say whether or not Goya did indeed, as verbal legend has often suggested, walk the streets and, for the first time in his life, at sixty-two, silently (for, presumably, being deaf he could have heard no shooting) see scenes of heroism and atrocity.

Some of the etchings in the series the *Disasters of War* seem to reflect direct observations; but perhaps this is less important a point than it seems. Goya doubtless knew of the horrors of war from eyewitnesses, even if he did not see them personally.

Did he see the flame depicted in *The Fire*? The picture is nonetheless realistic even if he did not do so. He felt, if he did not see.

But, at the very least in the two etchings of the *Disasters of War* entitled *I saw it* and *That also*, Goya is generally held to have been depicting something which he knew about – and perhaps in *This is worse*, Disaster No. 37, on which he noted the words 'the man of Chinchón' (*el de Chinchón*): Chinchón,

This engraving by Miguel Gamborino, done in 1813, provided the basis of Goya's *The Third of May, 1808*. In it we find the same opposition of two groups, victims and executioners: the monks shot at Murviedro and the firing squad.

a village to the south east of Madrid, had been given as a benefice to his brother by the Condesa de Chinchón, Godoy's wife and daughter of the Infante Don Luis.

He must also have seen how ironical it was that the very Florida quarter of Madrid where he had sketched picnics and dancing for his tapestry cartoons, should become a background for his most violent political painting. The hill of Príncipe Pío was, after all, only a short walk from the Albas' summer house, the 'Palacete de Moncloa', already bought by the King, and from the palace of the Duke of Osuna.

Further, as has been seen, the hill itself had been depicted by Goya already, on the left of his most engaging of *fêtes champêtres, La Pradera de San Isidro*, that ambitious canvas in the style of Velázquez which Sánchez Cantón (with some exaggeration) has described as Goya's 'only landscape'.

Finally, the church of San Antonio de la Florida stood just at the bottom of the hill, the other side of the French soldiers. May, too, the time of the executions, is the month of the celebration of the famous Madrid fiesta of San Isidro.

Goya in 1808 had been married for thirty-five years to Josefa Bayeu, sister of his onetime mentor in Saragossa. Of the Señora de Goya, almost nothing is known. By her, he had had several children (older biographies say twenty, modern six) of whom only one son, Xavier, survived, married by now with a son of his own, Mariano, born in 1806. Goya's father, mother and sister were dead, but his brother was still a priest at Chinchón.

About Goya's political views in May 1808 it is impossible to be precise. Did he, for example, ever believe, with the then captain-general of Barcelona, the aged *ilustrado* Conde de Ezpeleta, that 'Spain could only be saved by the Emperor Napoleon'? Goya's friends were men of the Enlightenment and several, such as the poet, Meléndez Valdés, Bernardo de Iriarte and Moratín, or the ex-Secretary to the Inquisition, Canon Llorente, sided with Joseph Bonaparte: Moratín became royal librarian, Iriarte and Llorente counsellors of state.

The creator of the *Caprichos* was evidently a rationalist; and the still powerful Inquisition and the ignorant and lazy priests and monks of old Spain were plainly repellent to him. But the shootings, the sackings, the rapes, and the brigandage brought to Spain by the French, equally obviously, judging from the *Disasters of War*, appalled him.

An old story (given some credence by its repetition by the distinguished art historian Enrique Lafuente Ferrari) alleges that Goya began his depiction of warfare the day after the shooting in Madrid: his manservant asked him why he painted the barbarities of the French. 'To tell men eternally not to be barbarians,' Goya is supposed to have answered.

It is also now known that in the middle of the Napoleonic war he set out with one companion (his wife by then being dead) to try and reach a 'civilized country'. He was sent back by police in Estremadura.

In the *Disasters of War*, as in the *Caprichos* and some of the paintings of the 1790s, not to speak of those of the time of war itself, there is an undoubted pessimism that contrasted with the hopeful spirit of the Enlightenment. The *Disasters of War* are not, to put it mildly, the work of a man who believes that human nature is essentially good.

Nor do all his paintings reflect anti-clericalism. In *The Third of May*, as has been seen, one of the condemned men is a friar; the series of paintings depicting Brother Pedro de Zaldivia outwitting the bandit Maragato shows a monk who is both clever and brave; Goya knew, of course, that Feijóo, who more than

Self-portrait.

The victims of the Third of May depicted in a 19th-century engraving.

anyone modernized Spanish thinking in the 18th century, was a Benedictine monk; and he evidently remained on terms with his brother Camilo, the priest.

Some of his religious paintings, such as the frescos in the church of San Antonio de la Florida (1789) or the *Last Communion of Saint Joseph of Calasanz* (1819) are of the first rank.

The probably conscious religious undertone to the composition of *The Third of May* evidently testifies to the fact that Goya, like most people of his age, certainly like most Spaniards, was never able to shake off the Church's hold, regardless of how much he may have had doubts about the truth of her doctrine.

There are, in fact, no exact records or at least none have as yet been discovered, about Goya's state of mind at this time. So his attitude to many of the happenings after May 1808 is a mystery, as indeed is his attitude to many other events.

Can the opinion of Malraux on the *Disasters of War* be really accepted? Namely, that they resemble the 'sketchbook of a communist after the occupation of his country by Russian troops'? For, whatever precise political feelings Goya may have had about Joseph and Ferdinand (and, like those of most educated Spaniards, it is obvious that they were at times ambiguous), it is clear from the *Disasters of War* that he was appalled by what he saw of the conflict: no one could draw the frightful *For this you were born* without a sense of outrage, less in respect of a particular cause than because of man's inhumanity to man.

Hugh Thomas
Goya, The Third of May 1808
1972

Interpreting *The Caprices*

Goya's contemporaries had no difficulty in finding political meanings in The Caprices, *though it is clear that there was room for more than one interpretation.*

All those who love the Fine Arts know of the celebrated painter Don Francisco de Goya y Lucientes. Many will have admired his fine frescoed ceilings, his Venuses and his portraits. But not everyone knows his masterpiece of drawing and engraving: the famous satirical prints which are called the *Caprichos of Goya.* The majority of ordinary people who have seen them take them to be merely absurd extravaganzas of their author. But those who have more intelligence naturally realize that each and every one of them contains some enigmatic meaning. In fact, this collection of eighty prints with more than four hundred figures of all kinds in it, is no more and no less than a didactic work of eighty engraved moral poems, or a satirical treatise on eighty of the prejudices and vices that most afflict society. All the vices are perceptively ridiculed in this extraordinary work – from those of the highest level of society down to those of the criminal classes. Misers, lechers, blustering cowards, ignorant doctors, skittish old ladies, dirty old men, layabouts and laggards, prostitutes and hypocrites, in short, all manner of fools, idlers and picaroons are so skilfully portrayed in the work that they give much food for thought to the reader, as he works out the subtle ideas underlying each satire, and in his own way and according to his own lights, finds more or less appropriate interpretations.

What more relevant satire could there be than No. 49, about the *Duendecitos* (Little Ghosts)! What truer or sadder picture of the effects of bad education than No. 72, in which we see vile men chasing and dishonouring a beautiful girl – one who seemed destined to be the delight of some family circle! What more fearful lesson than No. 59, in which a group of vicious people watches a tombstone of death in the act of falling upon them, as a result of their excesses. And yet no one mends their ways!...Their subtlety is such that even the sharpest minds do not perceive the whole of their moral point at the first perusal....

I feel that no other nation has a work of moral satire of this kind, or of comparable quality. Giordano's facility with the brush, or Ribera's anatomical knowledge, would not enable one to excel in this genre or compose eighty satires like these. One must have been born with an unusual mind, have had a wide experience of life, and have plumbed the depths of the human heart. Goya might have painted eight hundred portraits in the time he took to imagine and engrave this inestimable collection. Hence the unusually favourable reception which he received from the *cognescenti* of both Spain and abroad. From the ambassadors down to artists and travellers there is no recent arrival in Madrid who has not tried to meet Goya and obtain a copy of his work. All praise to Goya, who is an honour to his nation!... Many different uses could be made of this wonderful collection of prints. For beginners who wished to study Art, it could provide a superb introduction to drawing, since it contains a selection of ordinary human figures that are difficult to copy, and many distorted forms. There are more than 400 figures of men and animals... executed with Goya's unrivalled facility and wit.

Painters and engravers will find it a veritable text-book of their professions, given its infinite variety of heads, unusual situations, well-drawn dress, original faces, emotional expression and anatomical knowledge. Who else has engraved anything like this for mastery and dash? Who can rival Goya for audacity? Who has made better use of chiaroscuro?

Poets and men of letters will find in each satire a rich mine of ideas, to stimulate their minds and spark off an infinite number of moral reflections. Since it keeps alive and before their eyes the chief springs of human action, it can help them to maintain the level of inspiration they need for their own writings.

Finally, and most valuable of all, these satirical engravings reveal our vices in all their hideousness, and fustigate our errors as they deserve. From them we can learn to suppress the former and avoid the disastrous consequences of the latter. What greater use could there be in this veritable comedy of human existence?

González Azaola
Semanario Patriótico, 27 March 1811

A book of English-style caricatures on Spanish subjects has passed through my hands out here. It was published in Madrid about a year ago. There are eighty plates in all. One ridicules the Queen in the most forceful manner possible, and the allegory is so transparent that even a child could see it. In one of them a wall is falling, with a number of men underneath it, who are trying to hold it up by main force. At the bottom of the engraving the caption reads: 'And these madmen will not leave' (Plate 24). A third plate shows a tree-trunk clothed in a monk's habit. The sleeves have been slipped over two uncut branches simulating arms. The hood is pulled over the top of the trunk, and a group of good folk raise their clasped hands to this fine little god in an attitude of fervent prayer. At the bottom is the epigraph, 'This is what a tailor is like'. We might add, 'This is what Spain is like', where compliments of the sort are paid by Goya, who is painter to the king, and whose portrait has been placed at the front of the work.

Letter from Joseph de Maistre to the
Chevalier de Rossi, 1808

The private Goya

Between 1771 and the end of the century Goya corresponded with his close friend Martín Zapater, a prosperous unmarried businessman. These letters, a selection of which follows, tell us much about Goya's daily life, his dealings with the Court and notable figures of the time. Direct, humorous, illustrated with lively drawings, they show us a different side of the artist.

Madrid, 6 October 1781

My dear Martín, I am not in the frame of mind for poetry at the moment but I can assure you that you give me great pleasure with your poems; press on and even if I do not reply to your letters by return you cannot imagine the joy I feel when I get letters from you. Yesterday I bought some birthday presents for Manuel's daughter and I will send them to her by the first post, to her or to you, as being a trustworthy fellow. They consist of a pushchair, a doll with a fashionable little chignon and other trifles I can't altogether remember (I only know that they are things for the kitchen and the house), indeed everything they wanted to give me. Friend, your last letter was a knife in my heart: you can't imagine how I envy you the moment you mention shooting. God will not let me escape from here. For me there is no greater pleasure in the world. I have only managed to get away once and yet no one has done better: 19 shots, 18 hits: to be precise 2 hares, 1 rabbit, 4 young partridges, 1 old partridge and 10 quails. The shot I missed was a partridge. I particularly enjoyed my good luck, having set out with two of the best guns in the place. I won a certain reputation with them (who, I have to say, fired particularly well and between the three of us we killed a fair amount of game), but for this we had to go to the Sierra which is seven leagues from Madrid.

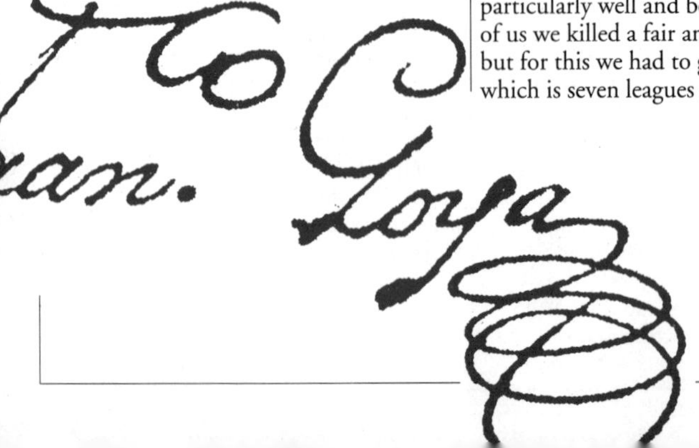

te se dar razon indibidual
lo q.e be adbierto el q. suelen
engañar a los arrieros con las
puertas. como me sucedio a mi
con q.e lo dispondras como quieras
e me informare yo p.r menor.

No ay mas no be
dades q. participar
a Dios memoria
nuestro
todos los
Palla
y a

Madrid, 30 November 1782

You must be saying to yourself: what an idiot, just from the way he squanders you can see it's not his money. I would answer that I am right, for why ask me to do your shopping for you if you do not want to receive what is best and in the best taste in Madrid. So nothing more needs to be said about Doña Joaquina's two garments; as for your overcoat, I don't think that you will have seen many as beautiful down there, for I had to move heaven and earth to find the cloth, having only seen it once before; it has therefore been very little used to make overcoats. Piran has had an identical one made, but in a ghastly colour, the cloth being so hard to come by.

Undated (December 1782)

Send me a thousand reals, in case, and keep your account, since you haven't decided to send me either turrrrrrones or turrrrroooones, or cakes from Tordelllllas, no matter, any more than the ddddog, nothing, nothing, nothing and now I can no longer remember what I was about to say, they are all talking to me at the same time, so that's all for the moment.

Undated

My dear, I received your valued [letter], but was beside myself to hear how the good-for-nothing Carrier of the Corset fulfilled his task; he must have kept it at home, or his wife must have worn it until she wearied of it, furthermore either you or I are drunk, or both of us, for I could not have told you the corset cost fourteen pesos as you claim in your letter since the box cost no more than eleven and a half pesos. It is the belt that cost fourteen, but they were copper reals, which is how the mistake must have come about.

16 December 1786

... Oh to be at your side and back in the plenitude we once enjoyed together! An end to applause, an end to marks of royal satisfaction! Full of solicitude for each other! But I cannot extend myself, I ask you simply to keep your friendship for me. I also thank you for the twelve sticks of turrón which were too much after the six for tea. By the same post I will send you twelve dozen chorizos, as for the receipt you ask for, tell me how I should draw it up, I have not the slightest idea, write sincerely to your extremely sincere friend.

Madrid, 15 August 1787

God willing your tertian ague will be cured by the pound of quinine I have bought you; it is the best possible quality, first class, and as good as that in the king's pharmacy.

23 May 1789

I have a son of four, who is so beautiful that people look at him in the street in Madrid. He has been so ill that I haven't lived for all the period of his sickness. Thanks be to God he is now better. As you are so gifted and so good at business, tell me how to invest a hundred thousand reals: in the bank, in royal bonds or in corporations, wherever it will bring me most....

23 April 1794

I am the same as ever; as far as my health's concerned, sometimes I feel furious, in a temper I find unbearable, sometimes I feel calmer, as when writing to you now. But I'm already feeling tired; all I can say is that on Monday, God willing, I am going to the bulls and I would have liked you to come with me, because of the other Monday, though there is an idiotic rumour abroad that you have gone mad.

Undated (1792?)

After I wrote to you someone bought me these four songs and four seguidillas in the form of a bolero. You must have them transcribed as promised, taking care not to make copies, otherwise the whole world would be able to have them. Those I have had transcribed onto a small paper are not very long. I have bought you two English knives in a case that also serves for sharpening them. I will try them before sending them to you. They cost me a lot of money, but are apparently even more expensive in London. They cost a hundred reals. I don't know if I was cheated, but I don't think so.

2 August 1795

Heavens above, so my pleasantries disturb you; for all their crudeness, they are quite a match for yours: you'll see, if you pay heed to them, that they will win through, because I am vain enough to think that only they perfectly describe the world.

You would have done better to come and help me paint the Alba lady who came into the studio for me to paint her face, and then went off again; I certainly prefer this to painting her on canvas. I am also to do a full-length portrait of her and she's coming back as soon as I've finished a sketch I am now doing of the Duke of Alcudia on horseback – he sent a message to tell me of the accommodation he has arranged for me there as the work is taking longer than I thought; I swear it is one of the most difficult subjects a painter can be faced with.

Goya in British and American collections

To appreciate Goya it is still necessary to go to Spain; few of the great galleries of Britain, Ireland and America can boast more than two or three of his paintings, and of these few are major works. They do, nevertheless, represent every stage of his career – the charming genre scenes of amusement and courtship, the powerful portraits of public men, the sensuous images of beautiful women, and the dark, occult side of his genius in scenes of witchcraft and satanism.

The Duke of Osuna, 1785, in The Frick Collection, New York (above) and *A Maja with Two Toreros* (below) in the Museum of Fine Arts, Houston, Texas.

The *Devil's Lamp* in the National Gallery, London.

FURTHER READING

Ferrari, Enrique Lafuente, *Goya: His Complete Etchings, Aquatints and Lithographs*, 1962
Gassier, Pierre, *Goya: A Witness of His Time*, 1983
—, *The Drawings of Goya* (2 vols), 1975
—, and Juliet Wilson, *Goya, His Life and Work, With a Catalogue Raisonné of the Paintings, Drawings and Engravings*, 1971
Glendinning, Nigel, *Goya and his Critics*, 1977
Gudiol Ricart, José María, *Goya*, 1990
Harris, Enriqueta and Duncan Bull, *Goya's Majas at the National Gallery*, 1990
Harris, Tomás, *Goya: Engravings and Lithographs*, 1964
Helman, Edith, *Trasmundo de Goya*, 1963
—, *Jovellanos y Goya*, 1970
Klingender, F.D., *Goya in the Democratic Tradition*, 1948
Licht, Fred, *Goya: The Origins of the Modern Temper in Art*, 1980
Malraux, André, *Saturn*, 1957
Mayer, A.L., *Francisco de Goya*, 1924
Perez Sanchez, Alfonso, *Goya*, 1990
Sánchez Cantón, F.J., *The Life and Works of Goya*, 1964
—, *Goya and the Black Paintings*, 1964
Thomas, Hugh, *Goya, The Third of May 1808*, 1972
Tomlinson, Janis A., *Francisco Goya: The Tapestry Cartoons and Early Career*, 1989
Viñaza, Conde de la, *Goya. Su Tiempo, su Vida, sus Obras*, 1887
Williams, Gwyn A., *Goya and the Impossible Revolution*, 1976
Wyndham Lewis, D.B., *The World of Goya*, 1968
Young, Eric, *Francisco Goya*, 1979
Yriarte, Charles, *Goya*, 1867

LIST OF ILLUSTRATIONS

All works are by Goya except where stated otherwise. The following abbreviations have been used: ***a*** above, ***b*** below, ***l*** left, ***r*** right, BN Bibliothèque Nationale, Paris, PM Prado Museum, Madrid

COVER

OPENING

CHAPTER 1

CHAPTER 2

CHAPTER 3

CHAPTER 4

CHAPTER 5

DOCUMENTS

Etching in *Tauromachy*
151a *'The spirited Moor Gazul is the first to spear bulls according to rules'. Ibid.*
151b *'The agility and audacity of Juanito Apiñani [in the ring] at Madrid'. Ibid.*
152 *'Pedro Romero killing the halted bull'. Ibid.*
153 *'A Spanish knight kills the bull after having lost his horse'. Ibid.*
154 *'One can't look'.* Etching in *The Disasters of War*
155a *'With or without reason'. Ibid.*
155b *'Nothing. That's what it says'. Ibid.*
156a *'There is no time now!'. Ibid.*
156b *'What more can one do?'. Ibid.*
157 *'It's a hard thing!'. Ibid.*
159 Miguel Gamborino. *The Shooting of the Monks at Murviedro.* 1813. Engraving
160 *Self-portrait.* Drawing, Indian ink wash
161 *Victims of 3 May 1808.* 19th century. Anonymous engraving. Municipal Library, Madrid
164 Goya's signature
165 Facsimile of a letter from Goya to Zapater
167 Drawing in a letter from Goya to Zapater
168a *The Duke of Osuna.* 1785. The Frick Collection, New York
168b *A Maja with Two Toreros.* Samuel H. Kress collection, Museum of Fine Arts, Houston
169 *The Devil's Lamp.* 1794–5. Courtesy of the Trustees, National Gallery, London

INDEX

B

C–D

E–F

G–K

L

M

N–P

Q–R

S–T

PHOTO CREDITS

All rights reserved 13, 27, 28, 31, 36–7, 37, 38, 44*a*, 44–5*b*, 72, 80, 83, 84, 85*a*, 94, 95*b*, 97, 104, 127, 128, 130, 131, 133, 135, 136, 137, 138–9, 140*a*, 140*b*, 141*a*, 141*b*, 142*al*, 142*ar*, 142*bl*, 142*br*, 143*al*, 143*ar*, 143*bl*, 143*br*, 148, 149, 150, 151*a*, 151*b*, 152, 153, 154, 155*a*, 155*b*, 156*a*, 156*b*, 157, 164, 165, 167. Artephot, Paris 46–7, 47, 56, 64, 70, 73*r*, 77*a*, 84, 85, 86–7, 98, 110, 115, 161. Artephot/Oronoz, Paris 39, 57, 60*al*, 68–9, 69, 73*l*, 77*b*, 79, 82, 87, 89*b*, 91, 100–1, 102, 103, 108, 109, 111. Bibliothèque Nationale, Paris 18. Bulloz, Paris 26. Edimédia, Paris 66*a*. Frick Collection, New York 168*a*. Gallimard slides 106–7, 118, 119, 120–1. Giraudon, Paris 63, 112–3. Image 3/Artephot, Paris 95*a*. Institute of Art, Minneapolis 126. Magnum, Paris 114*b*. Mas, Barcelona 19, 20, 21, 23, 32–3, 40, 112. Museum of Fine Arts, Houston, Texas 168*b*. National Gallery, London 92, 169. The Metropolitan Museum of Art, New York 69. Oronoz, Madrid 12, 76, 122. Prado Museum, Madrid front cover, back cover, spine, 1, 4, 5, 6, 7, 8, 9, 16, 17, 22*l*, 22*r*, 24–5, 29, 30, 48, 49, 50, 51, 52–3, 54–5, 58, 59, 60*b*, 62, 64–5, 66*b*, 67, 71, 74, 75, 88–9, 90, 93, 96, 99, 114*a*, 116–7*a*, 116–7*b*, 123, 124, 144–5. Prado Museum (Gallimard slide) 24, 89*a*, 125. RMN Paris 14–5, 61, 81*r*, 81*l*. Roger-Viollet, Paris 14, 78*a*, 78*b*, 132, 134. Scala, Florence 41, 42–3, 105*a*, 105*b*.

TEXT CREDITS

Grateful acknowledgment is made for the use of material from the following works: (pp. 130–2, 134) from *Goya and his Critics* by Nigel Glendinning, 1977, published by Yale University Press, copyright © 1977 Yale University Press, reprinted by permission of Yale University Press; (pp. 136–9) from *Saturn* by André Malraux, translated by C.W. Chilton, 1957, reprinted by permission of Phaidon Press Ltd, London; (pp. 144–6) from *Goya: The Origins of the Modern Temper in Art* by Fred Licht, 1980, reprinted by permission of Universe Publishing Inc., New York; (pp. 154–7) from *Goya and the Impossible Revolution* by Gwyn A. Williams, 1976, reprinted by permission of the Peters Fraser Dunlop Group Ltd, London; (pp. 158–61) from *Goya, The Third of May 1808* by Hugh Thomas, 1972, reprinted by permission of Aitken, Stone & Wylie Ltd, London.

Jeannine Baticle
is honorary head curator of the Louvre, having devoted her career to the department of painting which she joined as an assistant in 1945 after studying at the museum. An acknowledged expert in Spanish art, she has an extensive knowledge of Spain, its history and customs which enables her to situate the work of each artist in its social and political context. She has written several books on the history of Spanish painting and has a particular interest in Goya.

Translated by Alexandra Campbell

British Library Cataloguing-in-Publication Data

A catalogue record for this book is available from the British Library

ISBN 0-500-30042-9

Printed and bound in Italy by
Editoriale Libraria, Trieste